SINS OF THE MOTHER

Irene Kelly
with Katy Weitz

SINS OF THE MOTHER

*A heartbreaking true story of a woman's struggle to escape
her past and the price her family paid*

PAN BOOKS

First published 2015 by Pan Books
an imprint of Pan Macmillan
The Smithson, 6 Briset Street, London EC1M 5NR
Associated companies throughout the world
www.panmacmillan.com

ISBN 978-1-4472-9153-4

11

A CIP catalogue record for this book is available from the British Library.

Printed and bound by CPI Group (UK) Ltd, Croydon, CR0 4YY

Visit www.panmacmillan.com to read more about all our books
and to buy them. You will also find features, author interviews and
news of any author events, and you can sign up for e-newsletters
so that you're always first to hear about our new releases.

This book is dedicated to my wonderful partner, my four beautiful children, their partners and all my grandchildren – thank you for all your support. I am so sorry for all the hurt and pain I caused you but please know that I love you all from the bottom of my heart; I am so proud of you all. I also dedicate this book to my beautiful friend who passed away. I know you would be happy for me – I miss you so much.

Irene Kelly

LITTLE GIRL LOST

Little girl lost
Oh, where can she be?
Alone in the dark so no one can see.

No mammy to love her
no daddy to care,
as she sits alone
on the cold lonely stairs.

She hides behind a smile;
just a sweet simple child
full of innocence and grace
her dreams running wild.

She searches for love
but can no longer feel it,
they tell her it will come
but she no longer believes it.

They say first you must lose
then you will gain
but this little girl can't see it.
It's just pain after pain.

On a journey through hell
her life has no cost;
she has no name.

Just a little girl lost.

Irene Kelly

CONTENTS

⊤

IRENE

She is here. The little girl sits on the floor in the middle of the long dark corridor. I see her now but I can't reach her. She is all alone. Seven years old, she is crumpled like a rag doll on the cold tiled floor, thin white limbs outstretched under a tattered brown dress. Curtains of fine brown hair obscure her face. She is crying softly to herself. She knows no one is coming to rescue her, to help make the pain go away. She is trapped forever in this hellhole.

Over and over again I return to this place, to this same scene. The little girl on the floor, her face hidden in her hands, the sound of her sobs echoing through the long, empty hallway. The place smells of carbolic soap – it is cold here, always cold. Sometimes she looks up and then I can see her expression – it cuts me like a knife. Poor, tortured little soul, she is terrified out of her mind. She is hungry, frightened and miserable. But she deserves nothing less, she is told, for she is a horrible little child and this is where she belongs. Nobody loves her, they tell her. Nobody cares about her. Nobody is coming to get her.

But I care and I love her – only, I can never reach her. She cannot hear or see me – she is alone, totally alone.

Don't give up! I call to her. *I will come and rescue you. I promise.*

I know she can't hear my voice but I must try and make contact. Her terrible loneliness pierces my heart and the tears continue to fall – fat, silent tears that roll off her cheek and make dark spots on the tiles. I can't bear to listen to the sound of her despair any longer. I leave this place; leave the little girl on the floor. But I vow I will be back one day.

One day, I will return and I will find a way to free her.

1

JENNIFER
ͳ

The Long Way Home
MANCHESTER, 2007

'Bye!' I waved at my friends as they looked at me questioningly from the entrance to the grassy cut-through over the fields. I could see the confusion in their eyes but I ignored it and kept walking. I knew what they were thinking – why wasn't I walking home with them through the cut-through? If we used the pathway across the field, it was no more than ten minutes from the school gate to my home in a small cul-de-sac on the outskirts of Manchester. I usually did the same walk with my friends each morning. But the afternoons were different. I wasn't always so keen to get home, and today I really wasn't in a hurry. So I took the long route back up the busy main road, a route that added another twenty minutes to my journey.

The noise of the cars whizzing past filled my ears – it was just gone 3.15 p.m. and I ambled slowly, really taking

my time. Step, step, step. It was a warm September afternoon and I measured out the paces as my schoolbag swung
from my shoulder. Then I looked up to the small houses
on the other side of the road. On this side there were the
school playing fields where the boys ran around, hockey
sticks flailing. Their loud shouts and the referee's frequent
whistle carried over the flat fields. I felt a stab of jealousy – I
wished I had an after-school club today. Most days I managed to get myself into a club which meant I didn't leave
school until around 5 p.m. It was ironic – I didn't even like
sports all that much but now, at fifteen years old, I was
an enthusiastic member of the netball, rugby and cross-
country running clubs. Anything to stay at school and
away from my home as long as possible. So now I dawdled
in the street, stopping occasionally to change my heavy bag
over to the other shoulder. Some kids I recognized from the
year below emerged from the corner shop holding bags of
crisps and fizzy drinks. It would have been nice to go shopping occasionally, but without any pocket money there was
no chance of that.

I kept walking, trying not to imagine what awaited me
inside our small three-bedroom house. Since my older sister
Anna had left home seven years before I had effectively been
an only child, and while my parents were kind people, my
home life was, well, it was a little odd. I couldn't tell you
exactly what was wrong with my parents – the truth was,
I didn't really know – all I knew was that they weren't like

other parents. They were both from Ireland originally but had moved over here to Manchester before I was born. So while most of my friends had grandparents, aunts, uncles and extended families in the area, we had nobody. The funny thing was, my parents didn't even *talk* about their families. There were no pictures on the walls, no telephone calls and nobody talked to me about the past. Occasionally Dad would disappear to Dublin for a few days but when he returned he didn't tell me anything and I knew better than to ask. I was tired of being told things were 'none of my business' so I didn't bother questioning him any more.

A long time ago, when I was seven and Mum and Dad were both working full time, they had sent me to Ireland on my own during the holidays to stay with random aunts and uncles I'd never met or even spoken to before. This was a confusing time for me. Mum and Dad took me to the airport and I clung to them for dear life but they wanted me to visit my family and I think they thought it would be nice for me to have a holiday. Once at the airport, they handed me over to the air stewardess at the gate who accompanied me on the flight, and at the other end I was met by one of my aunts. This happened a few times over the next three years. I went to stay with my dad's sister Marie a couple of times and also my mum's youngest sister Emily, who had two children, but I was very quiet and uncomfortable at first. Mum and Dad never spoke about their relatives at all. They seemed like kind people but they were virtual strangers and, without Mum or Dad there, I was terrified. My despairing aunts would call my mother asking her why I wasn't eating or speaking to anyone. The truth was – I didn't have a clue who these people were.

This went on once or twice a year for a week at a time – but the gaps between each visit were so long that when I went out there again, I'd usually forgotten who everybody was. I'd only start to come out of my shell towards the end of each trip, and it was a relief when Ryanair stopped offering flights to unaccompanied minors. But it annoyed me that I had all this family in Ireland and I didn't know anything about them. I was too shy to ask them myself. I couldn't even say how many brothers or sisters my parents had each, let alone name them!

I checked my watch – 3.42 p.m. Dad might not even be awake. While my mum was usually a ball of nervous energy, Dad often slept in late and didn't emerge from his room until teatime. He'd never been an early riser but recently it had become ridiculous. I'd come in from school when he was just getting up and I'd leave in the morning while he was still in bed. Some days we hardly spoke to each other at all.

There was a time, many years ago, when we had been really close. I was a real Daddy's girl, following him around like a shadow. My mum had been married before and my two older brothers Justin and Philip, and older sister Anna, were from her previous relationship. They were all in their twenties now and lived in Ireland. I was my parents' only child together and there was a big age gap between me and the others so they hadn't played with me when I was little. But since I was Dad's only child, he doted on me. He was a practical man, a painter and decorator by trade, and he used to let me help out with all his jobs around the house. I never left his side and I loved it. He was a really good artist and he taught me how to draw. I'd help him with his painting, woodwork, gardening – you name it, we did it together. But as I got older something changed suddenly. It felt like he didn't want me around.

These days if he said he was going to do some woodwork in his shed and I asked to help him, he'd tell me no. 'You stay here,' he'd say. 'I won't be long.'

We barely spoke any more, except to argue. Dad refused to let me grow up. I was fifteen years old and, still, I wasn't allowed to go into town with my friends on my own, let alone to the cinema or, God forbid, parties. So instead, I signed myself up to all the after-school clubs, just to get me out of the house. I'd even had to fight him to let me walk to school on my own once I started senior school. And boys? Forget it! Lucas, a lad who lived across the street, was a friend of mine and one day he asked me out. I was dying to say yes because I liked him too, but I knew my dad would never allow it. He didn't even let my male friends come in the house – they had to wait on the doorstep. It was crazy – he didn't trust anyone.

He didn't even trust Mum or me. Dad had a habit of hiding all his stuff. He had a lot of secret compartments in the house and all his possessions were kept out of sight. So if, say, I wanted to borrow a book or his computer I'd have to ask and he would get it out of a hidden drawer that I didn't even know was there. All his stuff was secreted around the house in funny little hidden places. Did he think we were going to steal them?

At least my dad was predictable – sullen, strict, secretive and uncommunicative, yes, but predictable. With Mum, I never really knew where I stood or what mood she would be in from one day to the next. She had always suffered with her 'moods' – that was something I had grown up with. We all knew there were times that Mum would 'go under' – then she'd take herself off to her room and lock herself away for a few days at a time, not coming out to eat or wash herself. It usually went away after a little while and then she was back to her normal, energetic self. But recently the moods had worsened and become more frequent.

Right now, she was in the middle of one of her 'bad episodes' and hadn't left the house in about a week. She hadn't even changed out of her pyjamas the last few days and her greasy, unwashed hair lay lank against her face, while her eyes were always puffy from crying. The rare times she did leave her bedroom to go to the toilet her face was a mask of misery. I didn't know what made her like this or why she got so upset.

She often put her music on loud to drown out the sound of her sobbing but it didn't really work. I could always tell. And then there was the banging. I knew, I just knew that she was banging her head against the wall. But I couldn't do anything. The door was always locked. From the youngest age, these moods frightened me.

'Mum, what's wrong?' I'd call out to her through the door, tears stinging my own eyes. 'Can I help? Please open the door and let me in.'

But she never did. 'Mum, please!'

'Leave your mother alone,' Dad would chide gently from downstairs. 'She's having a bad day. Leave her alone now. She'll be fine tomorrow.'

Dad never seemed upset when Mum was like this – he was just stern with me, worried I might upset her further. It was confusing. I mean, I knew this wasn't normal, even if I didn't know what was wrong.

In the last few months, it had taken Mum longer and longer to return to her normal self again. I used to think it was my fault – that I had made her miserable somehow, though I didn't know how. I just wanted to make things right. But now, at fifteen years old, it didn't upset me any more; if anything it just made me resentful.

Why can't you be like a normal mum? I seethed silently in my head as she trudged round upstairs like a zombie. Night after night I came home to a dark, empty house. No kisses or cuddles for me, no 'here's your dinner, darling' or 'how was your day, sweetheart?' Nope – just silence. We were like planets orbiting around each other, never coming close enough to touch.

There had been one fun holiday, I remember, many years before when we had gone up to stay in a little cottage in Scotland for a week. I was about nine at the time and we went on walks on the beach every day and played in the sea. That had been lovely, and Mum and Dad had both been in good moods – there were no arguments the whole time. But apart from that, I didn't have any happy memories of my mum as a young child.

Further up the road now, a bunch of small kids swerved around me on their bikes, laughing and shouting to one another, weaving dangerously close to the cars. My heart lurched suddenly and then I felt a wave of anger. *What are these kids even doing out on their own without adult supervision? Where are their parents?* I would never have been allowed to play out like this as a child. That's partly why I was such a success at school. I was predicted good grades for my GCSEs and my parents had high hopes for my education. Well, I didn't have anything else to do so I had thrown myself into my schoolwork.

The only other time I got to leave the house was for my job at the weekend. I was a chef's assistant in the kitchen of a homeless hostel every Saturday and Sunday, from 8 a.m.

till 4 p.m. It paid £12 a day, which was just enough money to help pay for my bus pass and any extra bits I needed for school. Though as a family we'd never really had any money, it riled me sometimes that Mum and Dad didn't even have enough to get me the basics like books or shoes. Since we were on benefits, I'd long since given up asking them for money but I just couldn't work out why Mum or Dad couldn't get a job.

'Not right now,' Mum would shake her head when I asked her if she could get a small job to help us out.

'What about Dad?' I asked her then. 'Dad could get a job.'

'I don't think so,' Mum replied slowly. And that was it – no explanation, no discussion. If only they told me things occasionally, perhaps I could understand! But they treated me like a stranger.

When the opportunity came up to earn my own cash, when I was thirteen, I jumped. Mum wasn't happy at first but I soon persuaded her – after all, if they weren't going to give me money, they had to let me earn it somehow. And I loved working in the kitchen. For one thing, it got me out of the house. I'd already spent years dreading the long, boring weekends stuck at home with Mum and Dad. I'd listen enviously each Friday as my friends would describe their exciting plans ahead – trips with their parents to the cinema, a meal out or even a visit to their grandparents had me green with envy. I'd listen and smile, yet all the while a little voice in my head screamed out: *Take me too! Take me too!* We never went out together – my parents just didn't have the money. No, no – that's not true. We went to the cinema twice in my life: once to see *James and the Giant Peach* and once to see *Godzilla*. That was it.

It was all down to money, they said, but over time I began to question whether it was just that they didn't like to go out. It's not like they took me to the free places either, like the park, the library or the museums. Nope, that's wrong again. *Once*. Dad had taken me to the park *once* in my whole life. Generally, they were quite content to just stay at home. It was infuriating and mind-numbingly dull.

The only friend my dad approved of was called Rosie and she lived in the house opposite – occasionally I was allowed to play at hers but apart from that, most weekends were spent in my room going slowly, silently mad. So getting out every Saturday and Sunday was a novelty. On top of that, I was learning how to cook. This was useful since Mum had long since given up cooking.

There had been a time, many years before, when Mum made meals from scratch like stews, pies and soup. Her Irish stew in fact was amazing. But those days were long gone. Gradually, as my mum stopped cooking, my older sister took over in the kitchen and I would come back from school to her freshly made shepherd's pies or delicious curries so I didn't really notice at first that Mum didn't cook. But when Anna left home for good at nineteen Mum resorted to shoving frozen chips and burgers in the oven.

Dad only ever ate toast and bowls of cereal and Mum, well, she barely ate at all. She was thin as a rake and I almost never saw food pass her lips. She had short blonde hair and her face was very drawn so she always looked older than her years.

I was twelve when, fed up with freezer food, I started to teach myself to cook. At first, I made a lot of stuff from packets and tins, but thanks to my chef's assistant job I learned a decent number of recipes and started cooking proper meals like curries, pasta bakes, risotto and stir-fried noodles. I even tried to encourage my parents to eat with me, but neither seemed that interested. Mum occasionally tasted my food and sometimes she even managed half a bowl of curry, but she didn't have normal eating times so I started to freeze meals for her so she could eat whenever she was hungry.

Some days, it felt like I was the parent. Once upon a time they had both worked and I barely saw them because they had jobs – now, at fifteen years old, I was the only one working in our house, making the meals and trying to encourage my parents to eat. I wouldn't have minded so much but the stillness, the quietness of the house, got to me. At one time I longed for a baby brother or sister to play with. Each year they bought me a new board game for Christmas and every time my heart sank as I read the instructions on the side of the box: For 2 or more players.

Gradually, I realized it wasn't going to happen and, when I turned thirteen, Mum confirmed that she couldn't have any more children. It just wasn't possible.

I turned down the pathway that led between the houses on the main road. Large railings on either side instantly muffled the roar of the traffic. I wondered if it would be another quiet night tonight or if they'd be arguing again. Over the years, Mum and Dad had perfected the art of rowing and on more than one occasion I'd come home to find Mum's bags packed and ready at the door. A sense of glum resignation settled over me now as I emerged from the pathway and onto the quiet backstreet, turning left towards our cul-de-sac. I could see our end-of-terrace semi now, with its neat front garden and perfectly mown lawn.

One time Mum had actually left. It was funny because she hadn't said anything beforehand – there hadn't even been a big row.

'I'm going to see my friend Ellen today,' she'd told me casually that morning as I'd hurriedly wolfed down my breakfast before school.

'Mmm, that's nice . . .' I'd mumbled.

'I'll be back in time for tea.'

But Mum wasn't there when I got home after school and teatime came and went without any sign of her. By 7 p.m. she still wasn't home and I started to worry. I asked Dad if he knew where she was. He just shrugged in response.

So I went upstairs and, rifling through Mum's drawers, I discovered she'd taken half her clothes and her suitcase. Alarmed, I called my brothers and sister in Ireland but none of them had seen her. Anna seemed really panicked when I told her Mum had disappeared but Philip, who had always been closest to our mum, was calm and reassuring on the phone: 'Look, she knows what she's doing and if she needs to get away, she needs to get away. Just relax – she'll be back when she's ready.'

'Dad, aren't you worried?' I asked him that night. 'Mum's gone! She's taken off!'

'Ah, she'll be home soon,' he frowned, flicking the channels with the remote control. 'Don't worry about it.'

But of course I worried about it. Mum had never left home before and certainly not without a warning. His indifference was baffling. She was a missing person, surely! What if something had happened to her? What if she was in trouble and needed our help? Days went by and, despite the fact Dad didn't seem worried, I felt increasingly panicked and upset.

Finally, three days after she disappeared, the phone rang. 'It's me,' she said. 'Look, I just had to get away for a few days. I'm in Liverpool staying with a friend. Don't worry. It's not because of you and I'm going to come home soon. I promise.'

It was weird frankly that Mum even had a friend in Liverpool! She only ever talked about her one friend in

Manchester; other than that she never saw or spoke about anyone. But I had to accept what she told me and she was as good as her word. A week after she disappeared she came home but she didn't say anything. Both she and my dad acted like nothing had happened. It was maddening, as usual! I wanted to ask them what it was all about but I knew they'd just fob me off with something meaningless. On top of that, I was still worried about Mum's behaviour. The way she had acted was just so strange and out of the blue. I knew nothing about mental illness at the time but I guess I felt deep inside that something wasn't right with her.

I flipped up the latch on our wrought-iron garden gate and pulled it shut behind me before walking up the pathway towards our green front door. I wondered what lay behind this door today. Quietness, crying or shouting? Was Dad awake? Was Mum dressed yet? Had anyone bothered to make tea? I pulled out my front door key and fitted it in the keyhole. Then I turned it till it clicked and, hefting my shoulder against it, pushed the door open.

2

JENNIFER

The Call

'I have to go to Dublin – would you like to come?' Mum was standing in the kitchen with her back to me when I came in, her hands busy in a sudsy bowl of washing-up, her voice low and steady.

I was taken aback. It was good to see Mum up and about again – I noticed she'd showered and changed out of her pyjamas into a cream jumper over dark blue jeans. This was a good sign. But there was a tenseness to the shape of her shoulders and a taut, brittle quality to her voice.

'Sure!' I replied, picking out an apple from the fruit bowl. I was always starving when I came home from school. 'What's the occasion?'

I imagined it might be a funeral or a special birthday of one of the many cousins I'd never met before – perhaps it was a wedding or a communion? I put my bag down in the living room and shrugged off my coat, before returning to the kitchen doorway, munching on my apple, waiting for Mum to reply. When she didn't say anything I threw the core in the bin and opened the fridge, poking around half-heartedly, wondering what I might be able to cook for my dinner. Still, Mum didn't reply. She was slowly pouring the dirty water from the washing-up bowl and rinsing it out. I watched her well-practised movements as she wiped round the grey plastic bowl with the J-cloth then along the edge of the sink and, lastly, across the head of the taps. Then she carefully rinsed the cloth, squeezed out the remaining water, swiped round the sink once more then laid it along the tap to dry and turned the bowl upside down in the sink. The routine was the same every time and she expected the same fastidiousness from me when I did the washing-up. Once or twice I'd forgotten to wipe the sink and she'd been so angry when she'd noticed the water marks. She gave the tap handles one last turn, just to double check they were completely off and, finally, she turned to face me.

'Jen, a lot of things happened to me in my childhood,' she said in a calm, measured way. 'These things need to be put to rest. I need to go over there to sort it out.'

'Oh right,' I nodded. I didn't really understand at all, but I knew there was no point asking her to explain. Nobody ever really explained anything in our house. Still, I was happy to have the opportunity to go over to Dublin to see my brothers and sister and their families.

Mum said we were due to go over in a fortnight for four days – it would just be us two since Dad was staying at home to mind the fish. Hah! That was just an excuse and I knew it. Dad didn't like going back to Dublin. I wanted to ask him why – after all, all his family were there – but it was pointless asking him directly. I knew he wouldn't tell me. There was so much of his past that was a complete mystery to me and even asking him about it felt like I was breaking some unspoken rule. In the past when I had asked him questions he would dismiss my enquiries in an off-hand way: 'Oh, you don't need to know that – it was all a long time ago.' And then he never said another word. So I learned to keep my mouth shut.

'Why is Mum going back to Dublin?' I asked my older sister Anna, who was now twenty-four and had three children of her own. She had moved to Ireland like my brothers to be closer to their dad. Despite the age gap we had always got on well, and as we got older our relationship became even better. Anna was sometimes more like a mother to me than a sister and I felt I could talk to her about my problems. Now, we tried to catch up regularly on the phone but it wasn't always easy with her kids and my school schedule.

Anna was quiet for a moment and then she replied, 'What's she told you?'

'She said it's to do with her childhood and she needs to sort it out.'

'Right,' she replied. 'Well, it's a commission, erm, like a big investigation for all the kids who were in care in Ireland, just like Mum was. Some bad stuff happened to them while they were in the orphanage and she has to tell them about it.'

'Tell them what? Do you know what happened to her there?'

'No, she hasn't told any of us. But you know, this is quite a big thing over here. There are lots of children who were sent to orphanages in Ireland and some of the things they're saying now about what happened to them . . . Well, they're pretty terrible.'

I lay in bed that night as my mind replayed our conversation over and over again. There had been a lot of accusations of abuse in the news recently about Catholic-run orphanages in Ireland but I didn't know any hard facts. All I knew was that they were run by nuns and priests and that life was hard for the kids housed in them. That was it really. I'd always known Mum had spent some time in an orphanage during her childhood because her family were poor. She had never hidden that from any of us but she'd never actually told us what it was like either. I had seen the movie *Annie* so I just assumed it was a bit like that – not very nice but not dreadful either – lots of scrubbing with a bit of singing thrown in for good measure. The main thing that stuck in my mind was the fact that these children had no mothers or fathers. Orphan Annie, that's what they called her. So it seemed a bit odd that Mum was sent there, because she'd had a mother and a father when she was growing up.

'It's not just for kids with no mums or dads,' Anna had explained one night. 'Back then, there was a lot of poverty and sometimes you were put in an orphanage if your parents were struggling or if your home life was difficult.'

That was all I knew about orphanages, except occasionally Mum threatened to put me 'into care' when we were arguing.

One time when I was twelve it was particularly bad. Mum and Dad had stopped me seeing my friend Helen, who was in my class, because they thought she was a bad influence. Helen's parents were both drug addicts which meant they were very lenient with her, they never minded how long she stayed out or what she was doing. In fact, she could pretty much do whatever she wanted. She seemed so much more grown up than me, and she'd tried everything: smoking, drinking, snogging. She even had an older boyfriend and she got invited to hang out with older kids at parties.

Helen's world was so different from mine – so free and exciting – but any rebellion from me wouldn't go unnoticed. In the few months we'd become close friends, I'd got into trouble in school a couple of times for missing lessons and instead of coming home and doing my homework straight away every night, I'd spend hours on the phone with Helen. I thought everything was fine – I really thought I was getting away with it. Little did I know Mum and Dad noticed every tiny change in me and they weren't impressed.

One night I asked Mum if I could stay over at Helen's house at the weekend. It was a ruse. They wouldn't let me go to parties but I thought if Mum and Dad let me stay at Helen's house, there was a chance I could get to a party without them knowing. But Mum didn't even think about it – she simply barked 'No!' as if that was the end of the discussion.

'Why not?' I replied indignantly. It didn't seem fair that she had just rejected my suggestion without even giving it a thought. I didn't have any freedom!

Mum didn't say a word – instead she lunged towards me, grabbed me by the ponytail and pushed me forward, smacking my forehead off the fridge.

For a second I couldn't speak. I was dumbstruck – it hadn't hurt that much but the shock was terrible. A moment later she picked up the phone and brandished it in front of my face.

'Here's the phone,' she said in that quiet but very clear voice she used when she was really angry. She still held onto my ponytail and she pulled my head towards hers so that her lips were close to my ear. 'If you don't like my answer, if you don't think I'm doing a good job, then you can put yourself into care. Hmm?' Her voice quivered with rage.

'You don't *have* to be here, you know. I'm not *forcing* you to be here. Go and put yourself into care!'

I was shaking now with fear and shock. She'd really gone crazy this time! All I knew was that I had to get away from her – and quickly. So I twisted and wriggled my body until she was forced to let go of my hair. Then I ran up the stairs. But she flew up after me and by the time I had hold of my bedroom door to slam it shut, she was already half in the room, her face contorted with fury.

'HERE'S THE PHONE, YOU UNGRATEFUL CHILD!' she shouted. 'HERE IT IS – RING THEM!'

I flung myself down on my bed and screamed into my hands, 'GO AWAY! JUST LEAVE ME ALONE!'

And with that she stormed out.

I cried myself to sleep that night. The whole ugly scene had been so unexpected, brutal and unsettling. Did she really want me to go into care? What sort of a mum says that to her daughter? My body shook as I smothered my snotty sobs in the pillow, trying not to make a sound. I didn't want to alert them to my tears. It just wasn't the done thing in this household. Nobody showed their emotions, nobody got upset in front of anyone else. I'd been brought up to think that that sort of thing was best done in private. If Mum was crying she was always upstairs and away from the rest of us. I couldn't remember the last time my mum or dad had put their arms round me to comfort me. We weren't that kind of a family. None of us touched or hugged. It was all closed doors and silent tears.

When I was very little Mum or Dad used to tuck me up

each night and give me a little kiss on the forehead. But all that had gradually faded away around the time I was six – I didn't know why and I didn't ask. I just accepted that they didn't do it any more. We weren't ones to make a fuss over anything really. Christmas was always a fairly depressing time in our house – Mum didn't like Christmas so we didn't do anything special – and birthdays were usually marked by little more than a card. One time Dad forgot it was my birthday and when I reminded him, he walked to the corner shop, came back with a card, wrote it out in front of me and even had to ask me how to spell my name! I was so hurt by this – I was his only child for God's sake and he didn't even know how to spell my name or remember my birthday! I didn't let it show, of course – I didn't want him to know how much he hurt me.

No, we weren't a very demonstrative family. I had only seen my dad cry once in his life and that was a horribly awkward moment. Mostly, my dad was a blank – completely emotionless. If he was happy or sad we never knew about it – he always wore the same stern expression.

Two days after our big argument Mum and Dad sat me down in the living room and told me straight: they were banning me from seeing Helen.

'We don't like her,' Dad said, fixing me with his clear blue eyes. 'She's a bad influence on you in school and we don't want you going to her house any more. If she calls on you, we're going to tell her you're not coming out.'

I sat there stunned, an impotent rage bubbling up inside me. 'You can't do that!' I exploded. 'She's my friend. You can't just stop me seeing my friends. It's not fair and it's not up to you!'

'Well now.' Mum folded her hands in her lap. 'You're right – it's not up to us, it's up to you. If you decide to go behind our backs to be her friend, there's nothing we can do about it. But you should know, she's not welcome in this house and you're not welcome to go to hers. If we do find out you've gone behind our backs then there will be serious consequences.'

'That's so unfair – she's my best friend!' I huffed, crossing my arms.

'You'll find other friends,' Dad said firmly. 'Better friends than her.'

So I had a choice – I could carry on seeing her at school and go behind my parents' backs, but that would mean having to sneak around and lie to them. I didn't like that idea – it felt wrong. I'd never lied to them before and I didn't want to start now. For one thing, if I was found out I knew they'd come down on me like a tonne of bricks. I could forget going to my after-school clubs, my weekend job, and all the small but hard-fought freedoms I had won over the years. They would snatch that all away in an instant. I just knew it. There had been times in the past when they hadn't believed me when I'd told them I was with a friend and they'd called the parents just to make sure! It had been really humiliating and I didn't like the idea they didn't trust me so I tried not to lie to them. Reluctantly, I dropped Helen. It wasn't worth it, I told myself, I'd get a new friend. And I did.

Generally I tried to be a good daughter and do what my parents told me – it really wasn't in my nature to go against their wishes. But it was hard to live up to Mum's exacting standards. I sometimes wondered whether her obsessive cleanliness had come from her time in the orphanage. She was militant in some ways. It took me a long time before my washing-up reached her high standards and occasionally I would do something that would send her completely bananas.

One day, I'd left a mug up in my bedroom. It wasn't something I usually did – in fact, I kept my room really neat and tidy because I knew the consequences. This day – well, perhaps it just got overlooked in my rush to get to school that morning. But when I came home I went upstairs to do my homework as usual and was shocked to find she had dragged everything into the middle of the room. My mattress, duvet, books, clothes, make-up, jewellery – everything I owned! It was all piled up in a big heap on the floor. I just stood, dumbstruck, in the doorway while she came up the stairs behind me. She leaned over my shoulder then and looked into the room.

'You see, Jen? You *will* obey me and you *will* listen when

I tell you to put your things away otherwise this is the consequence.'

That night she made me put all my things back myself. And I never left a cup up in my room again. It was as if that one little thing out of place had sent her completely mad.

Just a week before we were due to fly to Dublin, Mum was worse than ever. She locked herself away most days now and her crying kept me up at night. Each morning I'd watch her plod to the bathroom, large purple shadows under her eyes, her tiny frame sunken under her dressing grown. Her torment was so raw, it was unbearable, but I'd run out of things to say to her now. She didn't want to talk, she didn't even want to look at me. Sometimes I wondered if she knew I was there at all.

At school, away from her, I wondered if she would do something stupid. Then, when I got home to find her locked in her room, crying but still alive, relief quickly gave way to anger. *I shouldn't be worried about my mother topping herself. I should be gossiping with her about boys and stealing her make-up! That's what other girls do with their mothers.*

Each day after school, as I turned away from the short-cut and up towards the busy main road, I'd turn away from my friends, from the ones who raced home to the warm embrace of their families every night. I didn't want them to see the jealousy in my eyes. I didn't want them to see how much it hurt. Inside, I felt cold towards my mother. I didn't care about the commission and what happened to her in her childhood. It was a long time ago now. All I wanted was a nice trip away. *What about my childhood? What about me?*

3

JENNIFER
⊤

The Redress Board

'Where are we going?' I asked Mum as we sped away from Dublin airport in the taxi. It was a beautiful, warm afternoon and, after a cramped flight, I was pleased to be out in the open and looking forward to seeing all my family. But when we got into the taxi, Mum had told him to go to The Cherry Tree B&B and given him a road name I didn't recognize. I was confused – if we ever came over to Dublin we stayed with one of my brothers or my sister.

'We've got a little guest house for tonight,' Mum said quietly, staring out of the window. 'Just for tonight, mind – we'll go and stay with your sister tomorrow.'

'A guest house? You mean, like a hotel? Will they give us breakfast in the morning?'

'Yes, they do breakfast,' Mum said absent-mindedly.

This was a bonus I hadn't expected! A trip to Dublin and

now a free breakfast too! I wondered why Mum was splashing out on a hotel room – she would never normally dream of doing something like this. She didn't even have money to pay for my school bus pass – how on earth could she afford a hotel? But I didn't question her further. I was too excited and I knew better than to interrogate my mother.

After ten minutes, we turned into a long, wide street flanked by grand Victorian houses on either side. Halfway down we stopped in front of a pretty, cream house with a pink blossoming cherry tree in the front garden. From the outside it was gorgeous – I hoped it was just as lovely inside. The taxi driver helped us with our bags and Mum paid him in euros, then we walked up the steps and in through the large arched doorway.

'Wow!' I was amazed. It was every bit as posh and elegant as I'd hoped, with a smart green-patterned carpet and chandeliers hanging from high ceilings. What an unexpected surprise! 'This is beautiful. Really, really nice. Isn't it nice, Mum?'

But Mum wasn't listening – she had started to talk to a blonde, middle-aged lady in tortoiseshell reading glasses sat behind the reception desk, giving her our details. My mind raced. *Why are we here? Why has Mum brought us to a lovely place like this? Is this a special treat for me? But why?* Oh, I didn't care about the reasons any more. I was just too excited and anxious to see our room.

A few minutes later the lady showed us into a large bedroom on the third floor.

'It's a family room,' she explained, holding the heavy door open for us. 'You've got the main bedroom here and then, through that doorway, there's the smaller single bedroom. The bathroom is off to the left there.'

I was practically bouncing up and down as we entered the large, high-ceilinged room with the big bay windows. I never expected to have my own bedroom! And it was so plush and luxurious. I ran my hand along the silky quilted bedspread and admired the corded ivory curtains. Everything was coordinated in subtle tones of cream, chocolate and gold, from the curtains to the carpets, to the wallpaper, the bedside lamps and even the cushions on the armchair. It was like a palace!

The lady was still talking: 'Now, breakfast is served between seven and nine-thirty. I hope you'll be comfortable here and if there's anything you need, please just ask.'

Mum walked in slowly behind me. She seemed to be very quiet today.

'Thank you very much.' She smiled at the hotel lady, who then left, closing the door behind her. I was so excited I could barely contain myself – I ran through to my room next door and marvelled at how I had my own TV and how nice everything was. Then I went into the brightly lit bathroom and examined all the free bath products lined up along the sink.

'Oh look, Mum!' I yelled. 'They've got little shower caps here! And nail files too!'

I rushed back into Mum's bedroom. She was sitting on the bed, staring down at the pattern on the duvet, her chin cupped in her hand. She was so still, so thoughtful – it seemed like she was a million miles away.

'Mum? Are you okay?' I asked hesitantly.

Silence.

After a while she sighed and looked up. 'I'm okay, love. Just, er, just having a little think about things.'

'Are we going to unpack?'

'I don't think we really need to unpack for just one night, do we? Let's just leave our things here, freshen up a little and go and see your Aunty Emily.'

Half an hour later, we were on a bus across town on our way to Aunty Emily's house. It was a gorgeous afternoon – warm, light and breezy, the perfect early summer's day. We didn't even have our coats with us. I felt on top of the world. Here in Dublin, I had so much to look forward to and a whole three days of holiday lined up.

'Well, now!' My Aunty Emily took both my shoulders to give me a big hug before standing back to admire me. 'Aren't you just getting more and more beautiful every time I see you!'

'No, not really,' I mumbled with a half-smile. My Aunty Emily was always very affectionate with me but these days I towered over her. She was only four feet nine inches and so slim and small! She had mid-length brown hair, full lips and a wide genuine smile. Everyone said I was the spitting image of her, which was a big compliment because I thought she was beautiful.

I looked around. Her place was immaculate – her husband Chris was a painter and decorator and their semi-detached house was always strikingly done up. They had a cream living room with a thick white carpet and glass coffee tables, and lovely pictures of the two of them with their two children – Fergus, who was the same age as me, and his sister Evie, ten – dotted about the walls.

I saw through the patio doors that Fergus was outside in their well-kept front garden and as soon as we sat down, Mum suggested I go out to see my cousin. It wasn't long before we were goofing around, play fighting, mucking about on his bikes and being stupid idiots on the trampoline. Mum, meanwhile, sat indoors with Emily, drinking tea.

The time just seemed to slide away from us and after a couple of hours of horsing about, Fergus and I sat down on the patio to get our breath back.

'So are you staying with your sis while you're in town?' Fergus panted.

'No, my mum got us a B&B,' I replied. 'It's pretty cool actually – I've got my own room and a TV at the end of my bed. And they do a proper cooked breakfast in the morning.'

'Wow!' I could tell Fergus was genuinely impressed. 'Why did she do that then?'

'I don't know. It's only for one night – but it's pretty nice.'

I glanced in through the patio windows then at my mum and Emily, who seemed to be locked in an intense conversation. Emily was speaking very earnestly, gesticulating wildly with her hands, while Mum shook her head. Even from here I could see she was gripping her mug so tightly her knuckles had gone white.

'Are you here long?' Fergus asked.

'Just three nights I think.'

'It's not long though, is it?'

'Long enough to get sick of your stupid questions!' And then we were off again, trying to wrestle each other to the ground. I was having so much fun I didn't notice the time go. By the time we left it was already gone 6 p.m. and I was starving.

It felt very grown up to get a ham sandwich in the 'guest lounge' of the B&B while the other guests enjoyed evening drinks and munched from little bowls of peanuts and crisps. I was tired now and grateful that Mum wasn't in a very talkative mood either. She'd barely said a word to me all the way back; she just stared into space as I wolfed down my tea.

'Do you want some of mine?' I offered her a sandwich. She hadn't eaten since lunch in Manchester airport's Burger King.

'No thanks, Jen. You have it. I'm not hungry,' Mum waved away my offer. Her quietness had returned but there was something else too now – she seemed more anxious than earlier. I wondered if it was something to do with her discussion with her younger sister. They had each snapped a taut 'Goodbye' at each other when we left. No hugs or kisses, barely any eye contact even.

'Come on, sleepyhead!' Mum smiled as she pushed herself up from the armchair. I had finished my sandwich and was now slumped, exhausted, in the gigantic cushions of the hotel sofa. After all the travelling, the fresh air and the running around with Fergus, I was so tired I could barely keep my eyes open. 'Let's go upstairs and get to bed.'

I made sure to have a shower and then I crawled gratefully into my lovely big bed just after 9 p.m. and switched off my bedside light.

'Are you going to sleep now?' Mum called from her bedroom where I could see from the flickering light she had the TV on with the sound turned low.

'I think so,' I replied, giving way to a giant yawn. 'I was going to watch something on my telly, but I don't think I can manage it now.'

'Alright then. Night, love.'

'Night, Mum.'

I closed my eyes.

'Hey, Mum . . .' I called out sleepily, a little smile tugging on the corners of my mouth.

'Yes?'

'It's been a great day, you know?'

'Yes. It has. Goodnight.'

'Night.'

I woke the next day to a room filled with dazzling sun-light. No sooner had I opened my eyes than I had to squint to stop myself being blinded. I'd slept brilliantly in my lovely big bed and now I had just one thing on my mind – breakfast! Mum was already up and showered so I quickly jumped in the shower and dressed in a hurry.

'Alright now,' she said as I came through to her room. 'Are you all ready?'

'Yup!'

'Right, well let's go down and have some breakfast.'

As soon as I opened the door to our room I could smell the frying bacon. I practically ran down the stairs and there, in the small dining room, was a long table covered in white tablecloths all laid out with a big breakfast buffet. There were large glass bowls with different fruit and cer-eals, croissants, bread rolls, plates of ham and cheese, and large silver tureens with lids that rolled up. I opened each of them excitedly: bacon, sausages, cooked tomatoes, mushrooms and scrambled eggs! There was even a funny grilling machine with a conveyer belt, which I found out from watching the other guests was actually a toaster. The lady with the tortoiseshell glasses showed us to a table on one side of the dining room and then we helped ourselves to what we wanted. I loaded my plate with bacon and sausage and toast then sat down opposite Mum, who came back to the table with a bowl of cereal and some fresh fruit. In that instant, I just wanted time to stand still. Right then, everything was so perfect, so lovely, I wished it would never end.

'What did you get?' I asked, admiring the little curls of butter in the cut-glass dish on the table.

'Just some muesli. And melon. They had two different kinds.'

'I've gone for a Full English!' I laughed.

'I can see that! Except here you have to call it the Full Irish. Anyway, make the most of it!'

'I intend to!' And with that I picked up the enormous silver cutlery and ploughed into the food.

We didn't speak much for the rest of the meal. Although she didn't seem in a bad mood, Mum was still distracted like the night before and she spent much of the time sitting back in her seat, holding her cup of tea with two hands and staring into space. I didn't mind – it was enough just to be sitting there together. I couldn't remember the last time I had sat down with my mother for breakfast. She didn't really eat in the mornings, let alone go to the trouble of making a fry-up. On the rare occasion we had a house guest she might fry a little bacon but I couldn't remember the last time that had happened. No, this was fantastic and I was going to make the most of every minute.

An hour later we collected our bags from the room and headed off to catch the bus – this time to Anna's house where we were staying for the next two nights. I must admit, I was a little sad to leave the lovely Cherry Tree B&B but still excited about seeing my sister and her kids. Mum barely spoke to me all morning – it was like she was lost in her own world. It didn't bother me. I was used to the silence between us and, besides, I knew all that would change once we got to Anna's house.

'Come here, you little squirt!' Anna enveloped me in a massive hug the moment she opened the front door. I was never that comfortable with physical affection – I wasn't really used to it – but Anna never took any notice of my shyness, in fact she positively revelled in my discomfort. I liked that she was so enthusiastic. Anna was a brilliant sister and we were the best of friends. She was thin like me with long dark straight hair – she was dressed in her usual uniform of jeans, T-shirt and Converse trainers. To put her and my mum side by side you'd think they were twins – they had identical faces. It had broken my heart when she'd come over to Dublin with her children, now four, three and a year old. As well as their aunt, I was their godmother and I felt close to them all. And nobody else made me feel quite so loved as Anna, even if it meant holding me in an awkward embrace for two minutes longer than strictly necessary.

'Let go!' I objected, laughing.

'No!' she teased. 'I'm just going to keep you here like this forever, my favourite little sister!'

'Your only little sister!' I corrected her.

'Right – for that you get another minute!'

'Oh, get off me!' I squirmed out of her arms only to be assaulted by my nephews, who literally knocked me off my feet. Sammy, the middle one, was shy like me and hung back, hiding behind his mother's legs. It always took a few hours for him to warm up and I gave him a conspiratorial wink before taking Liam down with a vicious tickle.

'Liam! Are you really four years old?' I said as he squealed with delight. 'Look at you! You're as tall as a house! I can't believe you're four. Are you really four?'

'Yes!' he giggled, rolling around on the floor.

'Are you sure?'

'YES!!!' he laughed.

The rest of the day was spent playing with the kids, catching up with Anna and generally enjoying the lively atmosphere of her chaotic family home. At teatime the table was laid out with a whole loaf of buttered bread and Anna produced a delicious home-made shepherd's pie. This was what I missed! This was a real family home. Even Mum seemed to visibly relax in Anna's house. There was always music on and Anna was as lively as the kids. I loved it here – it was noisy, distracting, messy and fun, everything a home should be. I was in bed by 9 p.m. as usual, sharing a room with my nephews, and fell asleep happy and contented.

The next morning I got up, showered and came down for breakfast where Anna was discussing the day's arrangements with her partner Donal. Donal, twenty-five, was the opposite of Anna: he was short at just under five foot while she towered over him at five foot seven. In contrast to her long flowing locks which almost reached to her bum, he had no hair at all. He had started going bald very young so he chose to shave it. Today he was dressed casually in tracksuit bottoms and trainers.

Anna had reminded me the night before that we were due to go with Mum for her big meeting today so she had got Donal to mind the children.

I grabbed a piece of bread and poured myself a cup of tea from the big pot in the middle of the table. Mum was still upstairs getting ready.

'Are you alright?' Anna asked.

'Mmmm-hhmmm . . .' I nodded, with my mouth full.

'Do you have any idea where we're going to today?'

I shook my head.

'It's called a Redress Board. They're going to speak to Mum about her experiences in the orphanage. She might get a bit upset but don't worry, it's all going to be fine. We're there to support her today, okay?'

I nodded. Soon my older brothers Philip and Justin

arrived to pick us up in the car – it was lovely to see them both and we all exchanged big hugs. Justin practically lifted me off the ground! At six foot four and well built, he was enormous and had a slow, heavy way of walking that made him look just like a lumbering giant from a fairy tale. Though Philip was just slightly shorter than Justin, he was much slighter and more sprightly, with a thin face and straight nose. They both wore their auburn hair in tight crewcuts and had on light blue jeans and trainers. It was Justin who announced it was time to leave and we all piled into his car.

Justin drove and Philip sat next to him upfront while I squeezed in the back with Anna, with Mum between us. Mum seemed her usual self – she hadn't made any special effort to dress up; she wasn't wearing a suit or any make-up. She just had on her usual jeans and jumper. Nobody said much as we drove – it was another lovely sunny day and I was enjoying soaking up the sights of Dublin. It had been ages since I'd last been here. It was still early in the morning and I noticed we had joined the throng of early morning commuter traffic. But while most of the cars were heading into Dublin, it seemed we were heading out. We drove out of the main suburbs until the houses started to fall away, replaced by country roads and large country houses.

After about half an hour we pulled off the road and up a driveway towards a large property set in very big and well-kept grounds. In the centre of the driveway was a lovely water fountain – the whole place looked like a very grand country house. Beside me I suddenly felt my mother's shoulders stiffen and I noticed that her face had set hard. I turned to look at Anna. The gravel crunched under the tyres until we came to a stop outside the building.

Now I could see there were other cars here and people milling around. I hoped this would just be over quickly so we could go back to the house and have fun again. Everyone looked so serious. We all got out of the car and Mum told us to wait while she spoke to her lawyer. She was off then, chatting to two very smart-looking men in dark suits.

'Just stick with us, okay, and try to be patient.' Anna put a reassuring hand on my shoulder. 'This could be a long day.'

I nodded to show I understood. I was grateful that Anna was trying to keep me informed but in truth I didn't have a clue what was going on. I wanted to ask her more but I had a feeling that she wouldn't tell me even if I asked.

'Right, they want us to go through here,' said Mum when she came back. I could tell straight away she had been crying – her eyes were all red and puffy, but she didn't give anything away. Instead she waved us into the building. At first we were shown into a large conference room with a big brown table in the middle surrounded by black leather chairs. We waited there as Mum went off to speak to her lawyer again.

While she was gone a lady in a smart grey trouser suit with a clipboard approached us. 'The hearing is about to start,' she said in low, confidential tones. 'Let me show you the room for family members.'

This time we were led out through a pair of patio doors into a little courtyard and through a long corridor. The lady with the clipboard led us into a small and stuffy little conference room with no windows. It was just the four of us so after a while we all relaxed and sat down on the black leather chairs. I hadn't seen Justin or Philip in ages so we passed the time by catching up.

An hour later Mum was back in the room – she looked worse than before. Her eyes were really red now and she had a drawn, pinched look on her face. Anna immediately got up and put her arm round her: 'Are you alright, Mum?'

'Yes.' Mum shook her off. 'I'm fine. Don't fuss.'

They sat down and spoke in whispers I couldn't really hear. I still didn't have a clue what was happening. Fifteen minutes later the woman in the grey suit popped her head round the door. 'Are you ready to go?' she asked my mum, and that was it, Mum was gone again. That was how it went all day long. In and out, in and out, while we all just sat in that small, stuffy room with no windows. Every time Mum came back in she looked more upset and exhausted.

It was such a confusing and intense day and because everyone was so solemn and serious I felt I couldn't ask what was going on. It didn't feel right – like asking who was in the coffin at a funeral. That made me angry. How come everyone else knew what was happening but not me? I was fifteen years old, I wasn't a baby, and yet it felt like I was being kept in the dark. As usual.

At lunchtime we had sandwiches brought to the room. Mum joined us but she barely touched her cheese sandwich. I saw the others were now looking really concerned and they tried their best to keep her spirits up but it didn't help much. Mum looked so sad, like a lost little girl. At one point she sat down next to me and I offered her a weak smile. I didn't know what else to do or say.

'You know, when this is all over I'll use the compensation to treat all of you,' she said to me. 'I'll get you something nice.'

I didn't know how to reply – I didn't know she would be getting money for this.

By the middle of the afternoon I couldn't bear to look at Mum any more. When she came back in after another round of interviewing, she looked so withdrawn and wrung out she had literally shrunk in front of us. It was a shocking sight. My sister and brothers rose as one and went towards her but it looked like Mum had had enough. She waved them away and collapsed on the nearest chair. Her face was ashen and her fingers trembled.

'I'll get you a coffee, Mum,' said Philip.

'Mum, are you okay?' Anna went to sit beside her and took her hand.

I felt helpless and a little scared. *What the hell is going on? I thought we were on a nice holiday – now everything is so awful and scary. What on earth happened to Mum in the orphanage to make her look like this?*

'You doing okay?' Anna asked me after Mum went back in. I nodded, but inside I felt wretched.

'Don't worry,' she went on. 'It'll be over soon. Mum'll be alright in time. It's just . . . upsetting for her, that's all.'

'What's going on? What's this all about?' Now I *had* to know. It felt like everyone was keeping me in the dark.

But Anna just clamped her lips shut and her eyes fell to the floor. 'Mum will tell you in her own time,' she said after a while. 'It's really not for me to say.'

I could have screamed at that point – it was so frustrating but there was nothing I could do so I just whiled away the time sketching.

Thankfully, by 3.30 p.m. it was over and we piled into the car for the drive back to Anna's. Nobody said much on the way home – Mum needed some peace and quiet, we could see that, so we didn't talk. I was in bed early that night, and grateful for the chance to finally close my eyes and forget about the whole day.

The next morning Mum went to visit Philip for a few hours while I stayed at Anna's, and in the evening Justin gave us a lift to the airport for our late-night flight home. I was sad to leave my sister and her family. It had been a short, confusing trip, not at all as I'd imagined it. The hotel had been such a lovely surprise, and of course I loved catching up with my family, but then everything else had been horrible and nothing was clear to me.

Mum was acting like nothing was wrong and, on the flight home, she was her normal self. Quiet but composed. But as we flew over the Irish Channel, something niggled at me and I couldn't help myself, I had to know.

'Mum, you know the hotel?'

'Mmmm?'

'Why did we go there?'

'The Redress Board paid for it – they paid for the flights too.'

'Oh – did you get things sorted out with them, Mum?'

'Erm, no,' she said, gripping the arms of her seat and staring hard out of the window. 'No, not really.'

It was nearly midnight when we arrived back at Manchester airport and we quickly caught a taxi back to the house. I was shattered and went straight to bed. The next day I got up early as usual and came downstairs in my slippers and dressing gown to make a cup of tea. Mum was still slumped on the sofa, fast asleep and fully dressed.

4

IRENE

The Bad Luck Girl

DUBLIN, 1964

'Monkey Face! Come here, Monkey Face!' I could hear my sister Frances shouting for me from the front doorway of our tenement block. I didn't reply. *Ha!* I thought to myself. *She thinks I'm outside but I'm not.* I was sat right at the top of the stairs, looking through the railings at my feet dangling below me. *And I'm not coming down! She can shout all she likes but I'm not coming down and I'm not going to reply either.*

I liked it up here – it was quiet and peaceful, one of my favourite hiding places. My other secret hiding place was called the cubbyhole, a bare concrete cupboard just outside our flat where we put all our coats. I liked to climb inside there and bury myself under the coats. I figured that if I made myself as small and as still as possible then I was practically invisible which meant that nobody could see me. And if nobody could see me, nobody could hurt me. Particularly not my mother.

My mother had never been happy with me, not from the very moment I'd been born. She never tired of telling me that she went into labour with me on Good Friday, and the pain made her cut herself with the breadknife. Bad luck, she said. I was nothing but bad luck – and my three older siblings were forced to agree. She was a cruel woman, my mother, but I loved her. So while I ducked her blows I still did my best to make her happy, helping her out with the cleaning and making tea for her. Anything to make her love me.

Today the cubbyhole hadn't felt like it was far enough away to be safe so I had retreated to the top of the stairs in our tenement block and hidden myself behind the tall black railings. My legs were so thin I could slot them between the railings and dangle them in the air beneath me, pressing my face into the wrought-iron bars. No one ever looked up from the hallway so I felt secure up here as long as I didn't make a lot of noise. Now I hummed softly to myself as I rocked back and forth on the palms of my hands, admiring my shiny black patent shoes. I loved my shoes; they were the nicest pair of shoes I'd ever seen in my life. I smiled at them now as I pointed my feet one at a time.

'Would yous stop mucking around now?' Frances called out from downstairs, pacing about in the courtyard outside. 'Just come back inside, would ya?'

Frances was the eldest out of the six of us – I was five years old and she was ten. Then there was Agatha, nine, Peter, seven, and Martin was a year younger than me at four. Cecily was still just a babe in arms. Our eldest brother Aidan lived with my granny on my father's side and we rarely saw him.

I held my breath as I waited for Frances to give up hollering and go back inside. She wandered around the bottom of the stairwell, called for me a little more, then finally shrugged and returned to the flat where I could hear my mother screaming. As the door banged shut I breathed a sigh of relief – I was tired of all their name-calling and their bullying. There were times I just needed to get away and be on my own.

'My name is Irene,' I whispered to myself. 'It's not Monkey Face or Skinny Malinky or Cry Baby. Or Bad Luck Girl. It's not any of those. It's Irene.'

It was my mother who had started up with all the names – she always used to say I was such an ugly child I belonged in the zoo. It hadn't taken long for the names to catch on and somehow the name Monkey Face stuck. Other times she said I was so skinny that if you lost your key you could fit me in the keyhole. They all laughed – I just wished she knew how much it hurt.

My mother Vera was actually a very beautiful woman herself – at thirty years old she was tall and slim with large blue eyes, high cheekbones and bleach blonde hair that hung to her tiny waist. She always dressed in tiny mini-skirts that showed off her lovely figure. Today she had hit me again. I didn't understand it – she never seemed to hit my siblings as much as she hit me. And I never knew what I'd done to deserve it – it came from nowhere and seemed to have no reason for it. She pulled my hair, slapped me and threw things at me. She did it with the others too but nowhere near as much. And they were never called horrible names. For some reason Mammy always saved up her really savage attacks for me. Today she had whacked me on the side of my cheek, leaving a stinging red handprint on my face. I put my hand up – it still felt warm.

'You stupid feckin child!' she'd erupted. She had struck me so hard the force actually sent me spinning on the spot. Immediately I started crying.

'Oh, what are you bloody crying for now? Jesus! You're such a cry baby!'

At that, Frances and Peter, who were sat at her feet, started to chant: 'Cry baby! Cry baby!'

'I'm not a cry baby!' I stammered, wiping my tears with the back of my sleeve.

'You are too!' Peter said and blew a raspberry in my direction. 'You're a stupid eejit cry baby!'

'Aye, he's right,' said Mammy, swigging on her bottle of Guinness. 'You're a bloody cry baby and I regret the day you were born.'

Her words hurt me more than her hand ever could. My

stomach shrivelled inside me and I turned cold with horror. I ran out of the flat and up the stairs to my hiding place.

Now, an hour later, and I was still up here. I'd calmed down a little but not all that much. At least the tears had stopped. I shifted my weight around – the cold stone floor had numbed my bum. I was far too thin – I knew that – but there wasn't much I could do about it. Food was hard to come by in our house and it was a daily struggle to ignore the constant hunger that clawed at my insides. Tonight was a good night; there was bread and dripping for tea. On a bad day there was nothing and if Peter didn't steal something we went to bed hungry. The stairwell of the block was very dark now with just a little light shining out of the windows of each flat onto each landing. I heard my stomach growl but I wasn't ready to go back downstairs.

We all lived in a small, sparse flat with just the two rooms, both with bare walls. The first room was the biggest; on the right-hand side was the window that overlooked the Liffey and underneath it was the settee. Past that was the fire and past that was the cooker. In the same room was a double bed where all us children slept. My mother slept in a small room at the back of the flat.

They're not your real family, I told myself for the hundredth time that day. *She's not your real mammy. One day your real mammy and daddy will come and get you and take you away.* I pulled my knees up to my chest and wrapped my reed-thin arms round my legs now. I didn't even know my daddy – Mammy said that he was working away in England but I never saw him. And according to what she said he never sent money home to us either. At night when she'd had enough drink and pills to soothe her violent temper she'd lie sprawled on the bed and curse him out.

'Never sends money back for us!' she'd spit viciously. 'What does he expect me to do? How does he think I'm supposed to feed you all?'

I wanted to go to her then and put my arms round her. I wanted to do something to make her feel better but it seemed I couldn't do anything right. One time I tried to hug her and she threw me off her as if I was a cockroach that had crawled onto her body.

'What the bloody hell do you think you're doing?' she'd shrieked, disgusted.

'I just want to help, Mammy.' My voice trembled with fear.

'Help? HELP?' she'd erupted. 'You can start feckin helping by cleaning up around here. Go on! Do the feckin washing-up!'

My eyes filled with tears as I slunk off to the large ceramic sink filled with dirty dishes. *Don't cry*, I told myself over and over. *Don't cry*.

'And don't bloody start your feckin weeping again!' Mammy groaned. 'Jesus, you drive me mad, you really do!'

I tried my best but the tears wouldn't listen and I started

to cry again. All I wanted was to love her and for her to love me. But she didn't love me. She really didn't and she didn't make any attempt to hide it.

Now I sighed and got to my feet – I knew I'd have to go back inside to say the rosary at 6 p.m. or I'd be in really big trouble. So I dusted my dress down and walked back into the flat. Luckily, nobody seemed to notice me as I came in that evening. They were sitting on the bed, talking. There was Frances with her thick, curly chestnut hair which hung down her back. She was the pretty one. Next to her on the bed was Agatha, who was well built with wiry, strawberry blonde hair and on the end, Peter with his mop of dark brown hair. He was a handsome lad but he had a quick temper and was always ready to defend our mother. I was hoping they might have left some bread and dripping for me and luckily there was a slice left on the chopping board. I looked around before I took the hard hunk of bread and started gnawing on it.

At 6 p.m. on the dot Mammy made us kneel to say the rosary with her – she'd been brought up by the nuns in the convent so she was very religious, making us say our prayers every night. It always made my knees sore but I never complained – none of us ever complained. We just got on with it, racing through the words as quickly as possible in order to get up off the cold floor and into bed: 'I believe in God, the Father Almighty, Creator of heaven and earth; and in Jesus Christ, His only Son, our Lord . . .'

Afterwards, I crawled under the covers of the bed with the rest of my siblings, all of us huddled under a big pile of coats for warmth, and fell asleep to the sound of their soft breathing. Sometimes, after a long day, my arms would ache. It was something I'd had all my life though I didn't know why they ached. Mammy always joked that I was lucky to be alive and she'd tried to throw me out of the window when I was a baby. The way she said it, it was to make other people laugh, but deep down I could never really tell if she was joking or not. That nasty little laugh at the end. *Did she really try and throw me out of the window?* I tried not to think about it. Instead, I closed my eyes and told myself: 'Tomorrow will be better. Tomorrow my real mammy and daddy will come and get me. And they'll never call me names.' I smiled to myself then and let the fantasy take me completely.

A couple of months later, just after my sixth birthday, we were given a new house in a council estate on the outskirts of town, again just opposite the River Liffey. Moving day was frantic – lots of the local families helped us put our furniture on a cart to get it across town. Compared to the tenement block, our new home was paradise. It was very clean and enormous – there was a living room, scullery, a separate toilet, bathroom, and upstairs there were three bedrooms. The front bedroom had two double beds and a single bed in it – that's where all us children slept – the middle room had a double bed and a wardrobe for my mother and the smaller room also had a double bed in it. The place wasn't decorated but it was large, clean and, best of all, there was a big back garden which led onto farmland.

On that first day I spent hours wandering through the fields at the back of the house, exploring my new environment. I loved being out there in nature, listening to the sounds of the birds and the frogs. Out in the open air, away from the clamour of the house and the constant shouting and thumps, I felt free and happy. Here I could talk to myself, sing to myself and just be myself. It was wonderful.

At home, Mammy didn't like us making a lot of noise – she said it drove her mad – so she made us sit on the sofa with our fingers on our lips for hours on end. And if we accidentally spoke or laughed then we were sent to our room with no supper. We had to be especially quiet when Mammy had one of her 'soldier friends' round. There was one soldier friend in particular who came to visit her a lot and then she would push us all out of the house and lock the door, saying we weren't allowed back into the house until later that day. I didn't mind being locked out all that much – I could spend hours sitting at the side of the river, throwing stones and watching the water speed by. Sitting there, I could get lost in my fantasy world – the world of my 'real' family, my soft, kind mammy and handsome daddy who loved me so much. I knew them so well in my imagination that I could summon them at will, picturing every detail of how they looked from their smart, colourful clothes to their beautiful, shiny hair. In my daydreams, they would dote on me, bringing me all sorts of delicious treats and sweets. They would dress me in pretty dresses, hug me lots and tell me how much they loved me all the time. They would say kind things to me, never tease me or call me names. And never ever hit me.

During the week we went to school on a bus – me, Frances, Agatha and Peter. The best thing was that we passed by a bakery every morning and they gave us warm, freshly baked crusts of bread as our breakfast. It made me happy. I liked school – it was a huge place, every room had dozens of children, and I kept up quite well with the lessons.

When we first moved in to the new house we had all our furniture from the old flat – beds, table, chairs, sofa, drawers – but as the months passed I noticed the furniture disappearing. When my older sister Frances asked Mammy where the table went one day she told her she had to sell it to buy food. That night I was careful to eat all of my stew because I knew our old table had paid for it – but I also noticed that Mammy had a couple more bottles of vodka than she had the day before.

We never had new clothes. I always wore my sisters' hand-me-downs, but they were so well worn that by the time they reached me they were completely threadbare. Kindly neighbours sometimes left bags of old clothes outside our door and we'd fall on these offerings, rooting around for something decent to wear. But often they were too big for my skinny frame or had been washed so many times they were falling apart. I adored my patent black shoes so much but soon they too were falling off me and eventually I had to tie elastic bands round them to keep the soles on.

One night we were sat around the fire when Mammy suddenly ordered us to shut up and listen because she had something important to say.

'Come here, you lot!' she slurred. She'd already drunk a couple of bottles of Guinness that night and her head bobbed unsteadily as she waved her arms at us to come closer. 'Come to your mammy now and watch – I'm going to take an overdose.'

'No, Mammy!' Frances cried. Martin and I just looked at each other, a little concerned but mostly confused. *What is happening?*

'Please don't, Mammy!' Agatha was in tears.

I didn't quite understand what she meant but I didn't want to upset my mammy so I just sat quietly. Carefully, Mammy opened all of the bottles of pills she'd been given by the doctor then emptied the contents onto the table. There must have been twenty or thirty tablets there – some were just plain white but others were little coloured capsules with tiny beads inside.

I didn't know what they were but Mammy always said they were for her nerves.

Now she rolled her fingers over them, almost lovingly, spreading them out on the table. She seemed to be deciding which ones she wanted to take as we sat there in complete silence, watching her. None of us dared to stop her as she picked one up, stuck it on her tongue and took a swig of Guinness, throwing her head back to make sure the pill went down properly. She did this again and again and again. Agatha cried silently while Frances and Peter just looked at Mammy with dismay.

Eventually, Mammy's head swayed, her eyes rolled back and she fell sideways onto the sofa.

'Quick, Peter! Come with me.' Frances jumped up. 'Agatha, you look after the little ones.'

Agatha nodded while I just sat there, not knowing what to do or say. I saw Frances and Peter run out of the house and heard their frantic knocks on the neighbours' door.

'Will you call the ambulance for us please?' I heard Frances beg when the door opened. 'Our mother's taken an overdose and needs to go to the hospital.'

I was scared and confused, especially because Agatha was crying so much. I wanted to comfort her but I didn't know how.

'What's Mammy done?' I asked her finally. 'Why is she sleeping?'

'It's the pills!' Agatha wailed. 'She's gone and taken an

overdose with the pills and it could kill her! Our mammy might die!'

At that moment I started to shake. *She could die? Why? Why has our mammy done that?* I couldn't understand it at all. Just then little Cecily started to cry from her cot and Agatha wiped away her tears with the heel of her hand, got up and went over to pick her up. She put Cecily over her shoulder and rubbed her back, making hushing sounds. I felt sick then. I just didn't understand why our mother would try and kill herself like that, right in front of all of us.

'Why?' I whispered. 'Why would she do that?'

But with the baby still wailing, the ambulance screaming up the road, the cacophony in the hallway from the neighbours and everyone still going mad, nobody heard me.

The paramedics were soon in our house, moving my mother onto a stretcher while seeming to try to wake her up.

'Can you hear me, Mrs Coogan?' the old, bald one shouted into her ears. 'We're taking you to the hospital now.'

But Mammy was gone – her mouth hung open, her eyelids drooped and her body was completely limp.

More than anyone, Peter seemed to be in charge of the situation. 'She took eighteen pills before she passed out,' he told the paramedics as they lifted the stretcher out of the house. 'She drank Guinness and the pills came from these bottles.' He handed them the bottles.

'What time did she pass out?' the paramedic asked.

'Ah, not long ago,' Peter shrugged. 'Fifteen minutes, tops.'

'Good lad! Now get the door for me, will ya?'

Later our neighbour came to look after us and, in bed that night, Frances whispered that Mammy was having her stomach pumped and not to worry because she'd done it before and it was all going to be fine. The next morning we were taken to stay in a children's home while Mammy recovered in hospital. Since I was still with my brothers and sisters, I didn't feel too worried. It was only for a few days and then we were all returned home.

Funnily enough, Mammy seemed much happier when she came back after her 'rest' in the hospital.

'Ah, it was just me nerves,' she said airily. 'I feel a whole lot better now.'

'You're not going to do it again, are you?' Agatha quizzed her. Agatha and I had been the most upset by the overdose and I also wanted to know that she wasn't going to do it another time.

'No,' Mammy said. 'I'm fine now. Absolutely fine.'

I wanted to ask her more questions – like why she had done it – but Mammy turned away from us then. That was the end of the conversation.

But she was never really fine and it wasn't long before she sat us down again, telling all of us that she planned to kill herself. As usual, she seemed angry and determined. I knew the drill so I didn't get too upset but still Agatha shook and wept with fear. This time, Mammy was out of hospital after just a few days. After the third time, it felt normal. Like the cold, the hunger and the beatings – it was just another part of life I got used to.

5

IRENE
᛭

Rags and Bones

'Don't forget to collect the sandwiches!' Mammy called to us as we left for school that morning. I was pleased to have joined my older siblings at our local primary school for the past few months. It was a relief to get out of the house and away from Mammy, especially since food had been scarce recently. Now whole days went by when we didn't eat anything at all, and the bakery had stopped giving us breakfast. Today I was going to class on an empty stomach as usual. At least at school we could rely on being fed at lunchtime. They gave us corned beef sandwiches. Today I was extra pleased because it was Wednesday – on Wednesdays we had fruit buns.

'Mammy, it's fruit buns today!' I reminded her cheerfully.

'Oh, whatever!' she replied. 'Sandwiches, buns – just

make sure you go round the classrooms after school and collect whatever you can find.'

It was one of the ways Mammy found to feed us when she didn't have any money. We would go round all the classes after school and stuff any leftover sandwiches in our bags. The teachers didn't seem to mind and I didn't mind either, even though they were usually hard and stale by the time we got them home. I was used to doing whatever I could to stop my belly from hurting.

If I wasn't at school I spent most of my days roaming the streets or the fields behind the house – I sometimes went with Frances and Peter. Occasionally some of the other kids off the street came with us but Agatha wasn't one for playing outside much. She preferred it indoors. Mammy was busy during the day, entertaining her soldier friends, and she didn't like us to be around so she'd put us out in the mornings with the strict instruction not to knock until we were called in. We were on the streets all day long but I didn't mind because they were wide, clean streets with big front gardens and I often played skipping games or 'piggy beds' with the other estate kids. Piggy beds was played with an empty shoe polish can filled with soil which we kicked onto numbered squares chalked onto the ground, trying to get the can onto each square from one to ten.

If I saw a crust of bread on the ground that someone had thrown out for the birds, I'd sneak it into my pocket and then go into the fields to eat it. When I was really hungry I'd go through the bins at the back of the estate – sometimes people threw out stale loaves or rotten vegetables. Peter often came back after a day on his own with a couple of loaves of bread, and when Mammy had a little money she made stew in the evening and porridge in the morning. When there was nothing else, there were usually potatoes to make chips – but not always.

On the few occasions when Mammy had some money she would send me out to the shops with Frances to buy the groceries. She'd hand us the list and the money and tell us: 'Don't come back without the money.'

At first I didn't understand what she meant so after we had set off towards the shops the first time, I asked Frances, 'How can we do the shopping if we don't spend the money?'

'Because we're not supposed to buy the food, eejit!'

'How are we going to get it then?'

'We have to steal it!'

'Oh. Oh right.'

Frances explained what we had to do. I had to pull our tartan shopping trolley while Frances held the shopping basket. We were to walk down the aisles together and she would put a couple of items in the basket but most of the food would go into my trolley. When we reached the counter I was to walk outside with the stolen food safely hidden in our trolley and she would pay for the items we'd put into the basket at the counter. The idea was to try and get as much as we could into the trolley without anyone noticing.

I was terrified of getting caught. I was shaking with nerves all the way round the supermarket as Frances casually tossed the butter, bread, tea and cans into my shopping trolley. She put the sugar and oats in her own basket and then, when we got to the counter, I walked outside. Frances, meanwhile, stood at the counter, calm as you like, as she waited to pay for the two measly items in our basket.

The first couple of times went like a dream and Mammy was pleased with us for coming back with the shopping and most of the money too. Trouble was, she kept sending us out to do it again and again and, of course, we got caught. Then the shop made us pay for everything in the trolley and they called the police. I was terrified as the large policeman marched us to our front door.

'What do you mean – *stealing*, officer?' Mammy clutched at her chest, pretending to be shocked when she opened the door to find us standing there shame-faced with two burly officers looming behind us.

'I'm afraid so.' The officer with the moustache behind me didn't sound at all convinced by Mammy's performance. 'Stealing to order, it looks like!' And he waved my mother's list in her face.

'Give that here!' She snatched the piece of paper from him. 'I had no idea they weren't using the money I gave them. How dare you make such a suggestion! I'm their mother, a good Catholic woman. They've been taking the money for the'selves, the little scoundrels!'

And with that she clipped me round the ear.

'Get inside, the pairs of you, before I give you a bloody good hiding!'

Frances and I scurried indoors, relieved to be away from the policemen.

'Now then, Mrs Coogan,' I heard them say. 'They'll get a warning this time, but mind, the next time this happens we'll press charges.'

'I understand, officer,' Mammy replied politely. 'And don't you worry – it won't happen again. I can assure you of that.'

She had not long closed the door before whacking Frances and me about the head.

'Ow!' Frances exploded.

'You pair of eejits!' she blasted. 'Why d'ya have to go and get caught? Now I can't send you out shopping for me again, can I? Bloody eejits!'

'I'm sorry, Mammy,' we both whimpered. 'We're really sorry.'

I was just relieved that we hadn't been taken to the cells and locked up in prison. It could have been so much worse.

The day they did take us away, in October 1965, I had no idea what was happening until it was too late. I suppose I should have noticed the official-looking men who came to our house the week before, poking around in our bedroom, asking us funny questions about what we'd eaten for tea the night before, but I didn't know who they were and nobody told me.

That morning Mammy said we were all going for a little walk and we all had to be on our best behaviour because we were meeting some important folk. So we marched behind my mother through the streets of Dublin until we came to a very large red-brick building. Mammy said Frances had to go with her but the rest of us were led into a small room.

'Now yous lot just wait here and don't be making a scene!' she warned. I didn't know what sort of a scene she thought we might make there. We just stood around, waiting, while lots of serious men in suits came and went.

After a while we were taken into a large room with high ceilings, and a policeman showed us to a hard wooden bench along the wall. We sat down and a man with a smart thin moustache, sitting behind a big wooden desk much higher than us, told us this was a court and then garbled a lot of strange words I didn't understand. He talked very fast and kept rustling papers so I couldn't really hear him very well: something about a court order, reports from people called 'social services' and then finally something about us all being made 'wards of the state'.

Mammy was in a different part of the room, sitting next to Frances behind a desk, and when the strange man asked her if she understood she just nodded, looking a little sad. I turned to my siblings – Peter looked stony-faced and angry,

Agatha, who was holding Cecily, was panic-stricken and Martin seemed as confused as me. At that moment a large policeman came up to us all and asked us to stand up and follow him outside. None of us moved.

'Come on now, children,' he said gently. 'There's no point making this any harder for yoursel's. Just come along now . . .'

'NO!' Peter shouted violently. In that instant, my mind flared with understanding: *They are taking us away from Mammy!*

'I won't go!' Peter shouted again and then got up and made to run out of the court, but the policeman was too quick for him. He leaned down and caught him in a big bear hug – Peter was struggling and shouting and in another second we were all up on our feet, bawling and screaming at the same time.

'Let go of me, you bastard!'

'I don't want to go!'

'Mammy! Mammy!'

'Don't let them take us away!'

'NO!'

'Mammy! I want to stay with Mammy!'

Before I knew what was happening we were surrounded on all sides by gigantic legs encased in black trousers – there must have been three or four policemen towering over us, their arms outstretched to stop us escaping. I dropped to the floor and started to crawl through a pair of legs, desperate to get to Mammy. Being so skinny, it wasn't hard to get through the legs but in another second a firm pair of hands dragged me up by the armpits and swung me out of the room.

'Get off! Get off me!' I screamed, my legs bicycling helplessly through the air. The elastic band on my left shoe broke and my precious black patent shoe fell to the floor.

'My shoe!' I yelled. I was crying now, tears streaming down my face, unable to comprehend what was going on, helpless to stop it. 'Please! Don't take me away. I need my mammy!'

All around me the air was filled with the terrible screams and wailing of my brothers and sisters as we were dragged, carried and heaved out of the courtroom and into police cars. Blind with rage and terror, I felt the cold Dublin air hit my calves. And still I struggled and still I called out to my mammy. The hands under my arms were too strong for me. I wriggled left and then right, I tried to reach for a face to claw at, I tried to kick out but I couldn't find anything. *Where are they taking me? Where is my mammy?* I screamed for her over and over: 'Mammy! Mammy! Mammy!'

Moments later, I was plonked down into the back seat of a police car and I looked over. Next to me was a furious Peter, shouting like crazy. My missing shoe was thrown in after me then Martin and Agatha quickly followed – they were red-faced with anger, howling their heads off. The car door was slammed shut, the driver started up the engine and, in no time, we were gone.

'Would you all just SHUT UP!' the policeman in the front passenger seat exploded once we had driven a few minutes away from the court. 'I've got your little sister here and she does not enjoy listening to your caterwauling. Just put a sock in it. It's not going to make a blind bit of difference anyways so have some thought for her and keep it down.'

It was enough to get us to stop shouting – I hadn't realized Cecily was upfront with the policeman. I didn't know what was happening at all. Martin squirmed next to me, Agatha sniffed and Peter punched the car door with his fist.

'Jesus!' he fumed, only quietly this time.

'Do you know where we're going, Peter?' I whispered but he just shook his head. I was scared now. I didn't know what to expect. We'd been sent to children's homes before but never like this – never from a courtroom. There was something very different about the way this had happened, very final. And Frances wasn't with us this time either.

The car wound its way through the streets of Dublin and for a while we all just sat silently in the back, watching the city fall away behind us, lost in our own thoughts. I was counting the minutes since we had last seen our mother, trying to memorize the streets we had passed so I knew how to get home. I bit down hard on my bottom lip and felt a familiar twinge in the pit of my stomach. I hadn't eaten for a couple of days and I was starving. Wherever they were taking us, I just prayed they had nice food. Or any food for that matter.

Finally, we turned off the main road and up a driveway surrounded on either side by well-mown lawns. The car slowed and then I saw on our left-hand side a large chestnut horse. It had been grazing but now it looked up as we passed by and I noticed a white stripe down its nose.

'It's okay,' I whispered to Agatha. I felt comforted by the sight of nature. 'It's going to be okay, Agatha. Look! Look – there's a horse there. They only have horses in nice places, don't they? So this is going to be a nice place.'

The car rolled slowly towards a huge, imposing grey building. The closer we got, the bigger it seemed to get and I could clearly see now that on one side there were the unmistakable tall slim windows and arches of a church.

'Are you sure?' Agatha whimpered as the car came to a stop and three nuns glided towards us. 'Do you really think so, Irene?'

I reached down now and carefully put my left shoe back on.

'Yes. We'll be okay. I'm sure of it. They've got a horse.'

6

IRENE

St Grace's

The policeman opened the door of the car and barked at us to all get out – now I felt scared but I tried not to show it. I didn't know where we were or why we were here but it wasn't a very friendly place. The three nuns standing at the entrance to the grey stone building wore very stern expressions. I'd seen nuns in church before but they didn't look like this – so big and severe, covered head to toe in black. And I'd never really met one in person.

The one in the middle, the tallest one, addressed us: 'Follow me, children!'

And with that she turned briskly on her heels and marched into the large building. They were all wearing black habits and I could see nothing except their black shoes peeking out from underneath and long black rosary beads hanging from big black belts at their waists. We had no choice but to run behind her as the other two nuns walked alongside us.

I couldn't believe how big this place was – I'd never seen anything so huge. As we walked through the corridor we were passed on all sides by children scurrying back and forth. They looked very serious. Some seemed to be carrying mops and buckets, others held books, but they all looked down at the floor and no one stopped to say hello.

At the end of the long corridor we came to a huge bathroom, where there were sinks and taps along one wall, another row of sinks in the middle of the room and, at the back, a row of shower cubicles. The whole place stunk of carbolic soap.

'Get undressed please!' the tall nun addressed us again. None of us moved.

Suddenly I realized Peter was missing and there was no sign of Cecily. 'Where's my brother Peter?' I asked. 'And where's the baby?'

The nun seemed cross with me and she sighed before answering: 'Cecily has gone to the nursery and your brother is being housed in appropriate accommodation for a boy his age. Now, no more questions – come on. Clothes off!'

We took our clothes off slowly and reluctantly – too slowly. The nuns started to grab at us and pulled our dresses and our vests up over our heads. I didn't like it. Then they told me, Martin and Agatha to get into one of the showers and turned on the water, which was freezing at first. We

were ordered to scrub ourselves with soap. I felt shy standing naked in front of these nuns. After we'd finished, we
were each handed a small rough green towel – it was so
hard it felt like we were drying ourselves with sandpaper.

'Ow, Jesus!' I exclaimed.

'Hush! None of that blasphemous language here, child!'
one of the other nuns chided.

'But it feels like my skin's being torn off with this towel.'

'Quiet – now come here.'

The nun had a big brush on her with some strange pinky
lotion which she started to paint onto each of us in big
strokes, covering our whole bodies. It felt really wet and
cold.

'What's this?' I asked.

'It's calamine lotion. Just in case you've got scabies.'

'I ain't got that.'

'You might. And you might have nits too – we need to
check you over.'

It seemed to go on forever – we were painted with the
lotion, still naked, then the nuns grabbed us each by the
head and checked our hair. Finally, we were each presented
with fresh clothes. I looked over at Agatha – she looked
scared stiff.

'Where's me old dress?' I asked.

'In the incinerator,' the tall nun said. 'It was filthy and
probably infested with lice. Put these clean clothes on.'

So we dressed in the new clothes – the harsh fabric of

the brown smock and green cardigan itched my skin but at least they were clean, like the nun said. I looked around for my shoes then but all I saw was a pair of dull brown T-bars.

'My shoes?' I asked.

'Gone. Put those on.'

Now I really felt like crying – I loved my shiny black shoes so much! But I managed to hold the tears back as I buckled on the brown shoes. I didn't like the look of them: they were so dull, so ordinary compared to my lovely patent ones. I waggled my toes – actually, they felt really roomy and at least these ones stayed on my feet. They weren't the most beautiful things I'd ever seen but it was nice to have a pair of decent shoes that were in good condition.

Once we were all dressed the smaller nun with the pretty face and pink cheeks marched us out of the bathroom and back out to the corridor. I knew it was getting on for teatime because my stomach was growling angrily. Children jostled past us now, and I could see we were all headed for the same place – the dining room. They were actually going to feed us here! But the moment we walked into the enormous room with the rows and rows of long tables with benches either side, my stomach turned over. *Oh my God – the stench! It's awful.*

At home there was a farmer who lived round the back of our estate and every few days he'd go round the street with his horse and cart loaded with two big barrels, collecting all the leftover food for the pigs. We knew when the farmer was out collecting the leftovers because the smell from those barrels was so strong and overpowering that it filled the streets and our nostrils even when we were indoors. We'd run around pinching our noses and screwing up our faces with disgust. It was rotten, just rotten! Now, in that dining room, I recalled that same smell. *So maybe those barrels weren't for his pigs after all. Maybe the pigman collected the food for the orphanages and the pigs were going hungry?*

We were shown to one of the tables and ordered to sit down as the dining room slowly filled up with children – there were loads of them, hundreds. I felt shy and embarrassed in my new clothes as I tried to keep my head down. After a little while a bowl of food clattered down in front of each of us. I looked into it. I should have been so excited – I hadn't eaten in two days. But the smell coming from the stuff inside made me feel sick.

'What is it?' Martin whispered to me.

'I don't know,' I whispered back. It was strange – like a grey, sludgy water. There were bits of stuff floating in it but I couldn't tell what the bits were because they were grey, green and black. It didn't look right but I didn't care at that moment; I was so hungry all I wanted was to stop the pain in my belly. So I picked up the spoon and started shovelling it in. It was horrible – worse than I imagined it was going to be – and I wanted to throw up, but I managed somehow to keep it down.

I ate really quickly and afterwards I sat back, hardly

satisfied but at least I had something inside me. I sniffed the air. *Mmmmm.* Something smelled good. What was it? Where was it coming from? I looked around me. All the children had their heads down over their bowls as three nuns patrolled the rows of tables. I leaned back slightly to get a better view. Now I could see right to the back of the room. There, at the end, was a table on a platform where all the nuns were sitting, eating their dinner. Even from where I was sitting quite far away I could see they ate from plates, not bowls, and on those plates were the unmistakable round shapes of potatoes sticking up. I squinted a little – they had golden roast potatoes, steaming orange carrots and some plump cuts of chicken too. In the middle of the table was a bowl – it looked like it had fluffy bread rolls in it. Ohhh, it looked so lovely, so good. My stomach started rumbling again. Now I knew where that delicious smell was coming from. But why did they have that nice food while we had the grey slop? I looked around, hoping to see someone approaching us with bowls full of rolls, but nobody came.

After lunch we were shown through to a large room where there were chairs all round the sides. There was nothing else there.

'This is the sitting room,' the small nun explained. 'You'll start school first thing tomorrow but for now you can stay here. The doctor has to see you later. Benediction is at six in the evening. I'll come and fetch you then. By the way, you can call me Sister Beatrice. Now stay there and don't make any trouble.'

'Excuse me, sister, what is this place?'

'Are you really that ignorant?' the nun sneered. I didn't know how to reply. Nobody had told us where we were so how was I supposed to know?

'This is St Grace's orphanage,' she sighed. 'Now enough of your stupid questions. Stay here and keep your mouths shut.'

The rest of the day passed by in a blur. At some point we were shown into a room to see a doctor who asked some questions and examined us and then, later, we were taken to the church for Benediction. Tea was a slice of stale bread and some watery cocoa then we were sent through to the sitting rooms – there were different rooms for the different ages. They were very large rooms with parquet flooring, high ceilings and wooden stacking chairs lined up round the walls. The three of us sat very close to each other but we didn't speak – we were too scared and confused. I just missed Mammy and wanted to go home.

Now there were children all around me, chattering and making a noise. I suddenly felt very small and shy. I just kept my head down and tried to stay as quiet and still as possible. Later we were shown up to the dormitories – Martin was in the boys' one and me and Agatha were shown to the girls' dorm where we were stripped and given a nightdress each. After we said our prayers it was time for lights out and I was so tired I closed my eyes and felt the inevitable tug of sleep. As I drifted off, my last thought was for Mammy. *I hope she's coming to get us tomorrow. I don't think I like it here . . .*

'Get up!' a timid voice whispered in my ear. Startled, I sat bolt upright. High ceilings, rows and rows of beds? *Where am I? What is this place?* For a moment I felt confused and then it all came flooding back. Agatha stood next to my bed, her sky blue eyes wide with fear. It was the morning now and I could see children bustling about the dormitory, pulling on dresses, rushing to and from the bathroom at the end of the corridor.

'We have to get up now!' Agatha whispered. I rubbed my eyes sleepily and looked around. Somewhere nearby I heard the unmistakable sound of a little girl crying, punctuated by the urgent whispers of another girl trying to comfort her.

'I'm sure she won't do it this time,' said the girl doing the comforting.

'She will!' the crying girl insisted. 'She'll put them up there and it'll be awful.'

'Ah now, crying won't help, will it? Is it *all* wet? All the sheets? Are you sure?'

'Yes,' and the sobbing started up again. I didn't know what was going on and Agatha was now tugging at my sleeve so I just jumped out of bed and got dressed hurriedly.

We were ordered to say our prayers once we were

dressed and then we had to go to the church for actual morning prayers. But just as I was walking down the stairs I heard the voice of one of the nuns shouting across the dormitory, 'You're a dirty, dirty girl! Look at you! Dirty!'

The girl sobbed but I didn't stop to hear any more. I carried on into church with the others. By the time we were done with all the kneeling and the praying, I was starving. We headed towards the dining room for breakfast. This time Agatha and I got separated in the queue and I ended up sitting next to some girls I didn't know. After a short while a bowl of porridge arrived in front of me. At least I think it was porridge. It looked like lumps of raw oats in dirty water. I plunged my spoon in and took a big mouthful. Jesus – it was disgusting!

I tried to chew but most of it was raw so it tasted like a mouthful of chalk. I chewed and chewed and chewed and finally I managed to swallow it all down. I took another spoonful and then a third. I felt ill but I carried on until I'd nearly finished it all.

A second later I felt a violent heaving in the pit of my stomach. I could taste acid in my throat. Then I buckled and the whole lot came back up again into my bowl. All of it. I panted hard for a moment and then . . . *Ow!* I felt a hard slap across the back of my head.

Sister Beatrice was behind me now, her cat-like green eyes narrowed into two mean slits.

'Eat it!' she ordered. 'I'm not moving till you eat it.'

What? Does she want me to eat my own sick? No. I can't do it. I just can't. I would rather starve. I shook my head silently and the tears started to fall. Fat, miserable tears plopped silently onto my dress.

'EAT IT!' she barked. Now some of the children from the other tables stopped eating to look at me. Agatha was at the same table but much further down so I couldn't see her from where I was sitting. I felt so terrified and alone at that moment – I just wanted it all to stop. I wanted to go home. I wanted my mammy.

'You're going to eat that or else.' Sister Beatrice leaned down now and spoke gently in my ear. It was scarier than the shouting. 'Or else – there'll be *consequences*.'

I didn't know what she meant but I didn't like the sound of it and I knew that I really didn't have any choice. I picked up my spoon and dug it into the porridge I'd just thrown up. When I brought it to my lips I could smell the sickliness of it and it made my stomach lurch all over again. So I held my nose, clamped my mouth round the spoon and swallowed. Urgh. It was horrible; the worst thing in the world. Again and again I swallowed the porridge sick until there was none left. My salty tears mingled with the vile food. *Why are we here? What is this place? Why are we being punished?* I hoped our mammy was coming to get us today because already I hated it in St Grace's.

After breakfast I was ordered to follow a nun who would take me to the school that was in our orphanage. By now

I was separated from my sister and brother. When we got outside to the courtyard I saw it was a grey, cold October day and once again I had to run to keep pace with the nun who was taking great big strides. We went through the courtyard and over to another building and after going down another long corridor, we turned into a classroom that was already full of children. At the front of the class stood an ordinary woman, not a nun, but she was the strangest-looking woman I'd ever seen. She had a very long chin and purple hair. She looked like a witch.

'Irene, this is your new teacher, Mrs Lawley,' the nun mumbled and then immediately left the classroom. Mrs Lawley was very tall and her long thin form towered over me.

'You're new here – who are you?' she asked, peering over the tops of the glasses that were perched right at the end of her nose.

'I'm Irene Coogan, miss.'

'Right, Irene, take a copybook and a pencil from my desk and go and sit down over there.' She waved her hand towards the back of the class.

I sat down and tried to follow Mrs Lawley's instructions. We were copying the letters of the alphabet that she had written on the blackboard at the front of the class. Normally, I was fine with my letters but Mrs Lawley had a funny way of writing. The letters were all curly and strange. I tried hard but as Mrs Lawley came down the row of desks she peered at my copybook.

'That's not right,' she snapped. 'Do it again.'

So I tried harder this time, being very careful to make the letters curl in the same way hers did on the blackboard, but I couldn't do it very well. Mrs Lawley was soon behind me again.

'No!' she said in a stern voice. 'No, Irene. That's not good at all. No wonder you're here. You're stupid. Come up to the front.'

I was shaking as I eased myself out from behind my desk and followed her up to her desk at the front of the classroom. She sat down then behind her desk and pulled out a long wooden ruler.

'Hold out your hands!' she instructed. 'Palms up!'

Trembling, I did as I was told and . . . *Thwack!* She brought the ruler down hard on both my palms. Oh God. The pain exploded over my hands in a white hot flash. Tears stung my eyes. *Thwack!* She did it again. And again. By the time she was finished I was sobbing really hard from the terrible, throbbing pain.

'You'll learn to do things my way in my class,' she trilled. 'Now go back to your desk! And stop your snivelling!'

I ran back to my desk and sat down, clasping my poor, hot palms in my lap.

'Hey.' I heard a little whisper from my left. Gently I turned my head to the side and I saw a little girl next to me with dark eyes, pale skin and freckled round cheeks looking at me earnestly.

'Don't cry,' she whispered. *What? Why is she telling me not to cry? I'm in agony!*

'It gets worse if you cry,' she whispered. I looked at her again, confused. She just shook her head.

It was all so hard, so confusing. I still didn't know what we'd done wrong to be sent to this place or how long we were going to be here before our mammy came to get us.

After school finished at 2.30 p.m. I returned to the main orphanage and was given a job for the rest of the afternoon. I was handed a bucket and a rag and told to scrub the hallway and the corridors. I nodded obediently and immediately got down on my knees and started scrubbing. In some ways, it was a relief. For a while I could just concentrate on this small task and not worry about all the other people in this place and the endless rules and praying. I worked hard, concentrating on just a little bit of the wooden floor at a time. It seemed like I disappeared into my own world because the next thing I heard was Sister Beatrice's voice.

'That's not right!' she said crossly. I looked up, terrified she was talking to me, but then I saw she was addressing the girl who was working in front of me.

The girl had been scrubbing away at all the skirtings but now she stopped and just kept herself very still, her head lowered and her rag in her lap.

There was silence for a moment and then a massive clang as Sister Beatrice kicked over the girl's bucket of dirty water. The grey water spread out everywhere, all over the floor we'd both just cleaned.

'Now do it again,' she sneered and she turned and walked away.

That night, I lay awake thinking about home and whether our mammy was missing us all. I wondered where they'd taken Peter and Cecily and how long we would have to stay here. I couldn't understand why the nuns here were so mean to us. Before now, I always thought that nuns were nice people. They were God's special people on earth so they were meant to be good and kind, like God. That's what I'd always been told, anyways. It just didn't make sense. None of it made sense.

'Budge up.' A little whisper came through the darkness and I felt the sheet lifting, letting in a chill breeze.

'Agatha!' I whispered. 'What are you doing?'

'I can't sleep,' she said. 'Please. Just let me in.'

I was too tired to argue. So, reluctantly, I scooted over to the side of the bed. Agatha climbed in and curled up next to me. For a fleeting moment, as I closed my eyes and settled down to sleep, I forgot about St Grace's and imagined we were back at home, cuddled up under the coats on our big bed. Mammy was in the other room, and soon our brothers and sisters would join us. As I succumbed to sleep, I told myself that tomorrow I would go and play out in the fields again. This was home, everything was fine and I was safe again . . .

7

IRENE

Ripped in Two

'Oh no. Oh no. No no no,' Agatha wailed, her hands over her face, her whole body shivering with fear. Agatha was four years older than me but for some reason I always felt protective towards her. She was soft and seemed so scared of everything. She looked at me then with her big eyes and I knew that this was something I had to help her with. On the floor in front of us lay the sopping wet knickers she had thrown off the night before. When I'd awoken that morning and seen them lying there I suddenly understood why she had climbed into my bed in the middle of the night.

'Don't worry,' I said quickly. 'Just go and get ready. I'll sort it out.'

As she ran off to the bathroom I ripped the damp sheets off Agatha's bed and replaced them with the dry ones from my bed. Then, as fast as I could, I put her sheets on my bed. Just in time.

At that moment one of the nuns patrolling the dorm strode past our row of beds – she caught my eye and I swallowed hard. I must have looked like I was doing something wrong because she stopped in her tracks. Slowly, she walked towards me and as she did, her eyes darted from the floor to my bed. She knew!

'Irene Coogan!' she addressed me sharply.

'Yes, sister!' I snapped to attention.

'Irene – tell me, whose knickers are those on the floor?'

'They're mine, sister.'

'And are they wet?'

'Yes, they are, sister.'

'And if I put my hands on your sheets, would they be wet too?'

'Yes, they would, sister. I'm very sorry, sister. I wet the bed last night. I'm sorry.'

'Get to the window!' she bellowed.

For a second I didn't know what she meant but then she spun me round and pushed me towards the large window that looked out over the courtyard.

'Face the window!'

I did as I was told – my cheeks burned hot with embarrassment as I realized that all the chatter and noise from the other children in the dorm had died down. The place was silent. The next thing I knew, sister had pulled up the window in front of us and she was edging a long wooden pole out of the window next to me. On the end of the pole were Agatha's wet knickers. By now the courtyard below was full of children running towards church for morning prayers but when the sister's voice rang out, everyone stopped and turned to look at us.

'Look at this girl!' she called to them. 'Look at Irene Coogan here. Look at this dirty girl. She's wet her knickers. Look at her dirty, filthy knickers! Look at them!'

The sister waggled the pole in front of me and the knickers bobbed up and down accusingly. I could hardly breathe. This was all my worst fears come true – I shook with shame as the whole orphanage, every single child, looked up at me. I wanted to disappear at that moment. *Please make it stop, please make it stop. Oh God, please make it stop . . .*

For the rest of the day, I could barely bring myself to look at anybody. I felt so humiliated, so utterly destroyed. I just wanted to disappear into a corner and hide myself away until it was time to go home, until Mammy came to collect me. *When is that? When is she coming to get us all?*

'Thank you,' Agatha whispered in the queue for breakfast that morning. I just nodded. I didn't want to talk about it. All I knew was that from now on we had to make sure that Agatha went to the toilet every night before bed.

At school I tried to keep my head down so that I didn't get the ruler again. My hands were still blistered from the day before and this morning's experience with the knickers had been a horrifying ordeal. If anything more happened to me at school I felt I would just snap like a twig. Fortunately, Mrs Lawley found another victim to harass in the morning and I managed to sit at the back without attracting any further attention. After another lunch of pigswill we were sent out into the yard for some fresh air. It was even colder today and my bare legs stung from the biting wind, but I tried to put it out of my mind as I stood against a wall, trying to make myself as small as possible. I wrapped both arms round myself against the cold. I just wanted to stay out of harm's way today, try to keep myself safe. There were so many rules in this place, it was hard to avoid a slap or a beating for five minutes at a time.

After a while I noticed a large gathering of children around a doorway at one end of the yard. I was curious. *What are they all doing there?* Before long a lady in a white apron appeared at the doorway with a big porcelain mixing bowl and a second later she tossed the contents of the bowl towards the crowd of children. A shower of bread rained down and, in that moment, the whole yard exploded into life. Children dived onto the scattered morsels, grabbing bits of bread, fighting each other for scraps, then running off to the other end of the yard. I didn't move – even from a distance I could see that most of the bread was green with mould. In no time at all the bread was gone and the crowd had broken up. Now all I could see were children hunched over or squatting in corners as they ate their bread. They shielded the bread with their bodies, as if afraid someone might snatch it at any moment. *Like animals*, the thought flashed through my mind. *They look like animals.*

Three days after I started school, when lessons finished at 2.30 p.m., I was sent to work in the nursery for the rest of the afternoon. One of the other children led me across the courtyard to a separate building where I was shown up the stairs and into a very large ward. From the moment I walked in, I was assaulted by the noise. The ward was filled with rows and rows of cots – about a hundred in all – and in each cot was a baby. A crying, wailing, miserable baby. I scanned the room quickly, trying to see my brother Martin and sister Cecily, but the place was too big and I couldn't find them.

'You! Irene! Get over here!' It was Sister Beatrice. There were two other members of staff and four older children like myself. With so many babies, we were hopelessly out-numbered.

'You're to change the nappies on the babies,' Sister Beatrice instructed. 'Every baby needs a fresh nappy and then it'll be the beds. You have to strip and change the beds and then clean the floor. Do you understand?'

I nodded but I was struggling to stay focused. All around me little red-faced babies were standing up screaming their hearts out – it wasn't normal crying either. It was different, like crying in pain. I went over to the changing table and picked up the first baby that I saw – a ruddy-cheeked boy with strawberry blonde curls in a long white gown. He was beside himself, bawling his eyes out.

'Hush now, little one,' I tried to soothe him. 'Come with me and we'll get you all sorted out.' Strangely, the moment I picked him up he calmed down – it was as if all he needed was the warmth of another person's touch. 'Poor wee man,' I whispered. 'You just need a cuddle, hey?'

I laid him down on the changing table and unhooked the pin at the front of the terry-towelling nappy. As it fell away I could see it was heavy with poo. Then the smell hit me. Oh Lord, it was like he'd been sitting there in his own mess for weeks! The poor boy had such a red, chapped little bottom that when I cleaned him up he bled.

'Hurry up, girl!' A voice at my side suddenly made me jump. I looked up to see a middle-aged woman in a nursery apron with a sour face staring at me. Her heavy-lidded eyes were framed by a mop of short black hair. She had rough-looking skin and thin lips. If it weren't for her massive breasts, I would have assumed she was a man.

'I'm trying,' I muttered.

'Don't give me lip, girl!' she snarled. 'Just do as you're told.'

One of the other girls whispered to watch out because this was Bernie, and she was one of the staff that had been brought up in the orphanage. 'She's not a nun,' said the girl as we emptied soiled nappies together. 'But she's just as mean. Sometimes even worse.'

For hours and hours I stood at the changing table, dealing with one bawling baby after another. Sometimes I tried to hold the babies for a little and rock them, just to give them some comfort. But if Bernie caught me holding them she'd shout at me not to dawdle.

At one point a terrible piercing cry rang through the nursery. Automatically I looked up and around to see where the cry came from. A second shriek drew my eye to Sister Beatrice who had a child laid down on another changing table.

She was doing something to a little girl, putting something inside her. I squinted to get a better look. *What is going on? What is she doing?* Whatever it was, that child was in terrible pain. As I squinted, Sister Beatrice looked up and caught my eye. She gave me such a fearsome look that I hurriedly turned back to my work.

I hated it in the nursery. There was something very wrong about the way the nuns and staff dealt with the babies, as if they weren't people at all. But I didn't have any choice – I was sent to work there every day after school and on the weekends too. At the start of my second week in St Grace's it felt like I'd been there for a lifetime already, and my hopes of being rescued by Mammy were fading every day.

'She'd come to get us if she could,' Agatha reasoned one evening.

'But what if she's not allowed?' I said. 'Maybe we'll have to be here for the rest of our lives. I don't think I could stand it, Aggie. I hate it here.'

'Don't worry,' Agatha replied. 'She'll come for us. You'll see.'

But by the third week I was desperately unhappy. One morning, I walked into the nursery to be met by the sound of my brother Martin crying with pain. I knew it was him straight away – even above the ordinary cries of the other babies, I recognized my brother's cries. I ran over to where I saw Bernie had him on a changing table – my brother still wore a nappy at night – and then I caught sight of something I didn't like at all. Bernie had the nappy pin open and there was blood coming out of my brother's back passage. I didn't understand it – why was Bernie trying to hurt my brother like this? For a minute, I just stood there, unwilling to believe my own eyes. Was she putting it inside him? She was! As soon as I'd recovered from the shock, I started shouting at the top of my voice: 'STOP! STOP! YOU'RE HURTING HIM!'

She whipped round and gave me an evil look, then she pretended I wasn't there and carried on putting on Martin's nappy.

'That's right – all done!' she exclaimed brightly.

She quickly tied up the nappy at the front, put the nappy

pin in to secure it then helped Martin off the table. He winced as he moved away but he wouldn't look me in the eye. I wanted to ask her what she had done but I was too frightened.

I shook with emotion. *What are they doing to the children here?*

It wasn't right. It just wasn't right. I knew it in my heart – the place was run by nuns but what they were doing to the babies was ungodly. It was bad and sinful. I knew that much. Each day I left the nursery with a heavy heart and the sound of the wailing still ringing in my ears. I hated the thought of leaving Cecily and Martin in that place. The nuns and the staff were so cruel to the little ones who were helpless to stop them. It was bad enough for me and I was six!

The following Saturday morning I was back in the nursery, dashing around trying to get all the toddlers onto the potties. Agatha was also there and we hadn't been at work long before I heard her crying.

'Irene!' she called out quietly, obviously trying not to attract the attention of the nuns and the staff on the ward.

I scurried over to the corner where I saw she had our sister Cecily on the floor fully dressed except she had one shoe on; the other was in Agatha's hand.

'What is it?' I whispered. 'What's wrong?'

'I can't get Cecily's shoe on!' she sobbed. She held out the little burgundy buckle-up shoe towards me and I took it. I had a go myself but it was soon clear that Cecily's left foot was too swollen to get the shoe to fit. Confused, I took off the right shoe then peeled down Cecily's tights. To my shock I saw that the whole of her left foot was one big, angry, red blister.

'It's burnt!' I exclaimed. 'Her foot is burnt!'

Agatha gasped with shock and now Cecily started crying. I could see she was in a lot of pain.

'Was it the hot-water bottle?' I asked Cecily and she nodded. The nuns put a hot-water bottle in the cots with the babies every night to keep them warm. Someone had put a hot-water bottle directly onto Cecily's foot and left her like that all night long!

'Please, sister!' I called out to Sister Beatrice, who was in the middle of the room.

'What is it?' she answered tersely.

'I think my sister has been hurt,' I said. 'Look at her foot. It's blistered and we can't get the shoe on it. Should I take her to see the nurse?'

'No, don't be stupid, child. Just push the shoe onto her. I'm sure it's fine.'

Then she walked away. Agatha looked at me with despair but there was nothing we could do.

The next day I discovered I was so hungry I had no choice. After lunch, when we were put out to the yard, I went to the doorway to wait with the other children. When the lady with the bowl came out I made sure I dived headfirst onto a piece of mouldy roll. Then I scampered off to the far end of the yard and pushed myself into a corner, crouching down low so nobody could see me. I knew the drill. I had seen children snatch and steal pieces of bread from one another so I had to make sure I ate it quickly. There, I tore off chunks of stale bread and gulped them down, grateful to stop the terrible pangs of hunger that now left me doubled over in agony. Afterwards, I felt strangely numb. I had seen the children do the same thing a few weeks before and I remembered thinking how they looked like animals. Now I was an animal too. *What is happening to me? What is going on?* Nothing made sense any more.

At the nursery I saw the nuns doing that thing with the nappy pins to more and more children and it made me feel so awful I couldn't sleep at night. It was the start of a new week and Bernie called me over one afternoon and ordered me to strip.

'What for?' I asked. I didn't like the sound of this.

'Don't argue, girl!' she snapped. 'Do you want to be sent to the Mother Superior?'

I shook my head, no. The Mother Superior was the head nun. I hadn't had much to do with her yet but I had heard how she beat children with a belt. I definitely did not want to go and see her so I did as I was told. Bernie told me to take off my knickers and dress and lay back on the wide windowsill which was two feet off the ground. Then she put the pin inside my privates. I knew the pin was open because I felt a terrible sharp pain. A second later she yanked it out again – Oh Christ! It was like she was ripping out my insides.

I screamed in agony and then immediately drew up my knees to my chest and rolled onto the floor, hugging myself and crying in pain. *Why? Why are they doing this to us?* I didn't understand any of it. All I knew was I had to make it stop.

The next morning, as the dorm came to life, I rolled out of bed and winced slightly as I felt a soreness down below from what Bernie had done to me. I crawled over to Agatha, who was still asleep, and nudged her impatiently – I'd barely slept a wink all night from the pain and I was relieved to finally get up.

'Come on,' I whispered. 'Let's go back home.'

'What?' Agatha mumbled, still dumb with sleep. 'What do you mean?'

'I mean it's not far from here and if we got back home, there's nothing they could do about it.'

There was a pause.

'Won't we get into trouble?'

'This place . . .' I sighed and rolled my eyes. 'You're always in trouble here anyways! It doesn't matter what you do. I hate it, Agatha. I can't stay any longer. If we get home and tell Mammy what's happening she won't make us go back.'

Agatha locked eyes with me then – I saw in that moment she felt the same way and she nodded. We dressed quickly and tried to make ourselves small and quiet so that nobody would notice us. We went to morning prayers as usual and then afterwards we snuck into the nursery to get Martin.

'What about Cecily?' he asked. I shook my head sadly.

'Her foot is burnt – she can't walk!' Agatha explained.

'Look, we'll just have to make Mammy come and get Cecily once we are back home,' I said. 'We can't take her now – we can't carry her all the way back.'

By now most of the other children were rushing from the church and into the dining hall for breakfast. We followed the line but instead of turning up the corridor which led to the dining hall, we went straight on, towards the front door that led out to the driveway, the paddock and beyond. There were no nuns around and Agatha and I held hands with Martin, who walked between the two of us. My heart was hammering like crazy inside my chest but I tried to stay calm. All I wanted now was to go home and see Mammy. Beside me I heard the footsteps of my brother and sister. I heard Agatha's footsteps speed up and felt a little tug as she hurried on towards the front door. She was panicking.

'Just go slowly,' I whispered. 'Don't worry – I don't see any nuns. Just keep walking and we'll be out really soon.'

It felt like forever but eventually we emerged onto the driveway we had travelled up almost a month earlier. It had been the worst month of my life and now I just wanted it all to go away.

Once we were out in the open air, I quickened my pace. 'Come on!' I urged the other two. 'Let's run!'

And the three of us, hand in hand, ran all the way down that long driveway, past the grazing chestnut horse with the white stripe and away from all the nuns in St Grace's. A few minutes later we popped out onto the main road. Excited, I turned to my brother and sister and, for the first time since we passed through those gates, we all smiled.

8

IRENE

A Way Out

I had a funny feeling about the police car that rolled down the road beside us. The way it was moving, it was going too slow. *A car doesn't normally crawl along*, I thought. They were looking for someone. We were walking now at a steady pace and though every fibre of my being wanted to run, I knew that if we sprinted away from the car, it would only attract attention. When it pulled up alongside us and I saw a nun in the front seat, I knew it was all over.

'Irene! Agatha! Martin!' the nun addressed us briskly.

We all stopped dead and looked at her now. But none of us moved.

'Come on now, children.' The nun began to fuss as she got out of the car and opened the back door, herding us all towards it. I could have run at that point but I knew it was useless. They would catch up with me too quickly. My heart sank as I realized my plan had failed. We had been gone fifteen minutes at most! Agatha looked at me with tears in her eyes. I turned away. I couldn't bear the fact that we were trapped in St Grace's and there was nothing we could do to escape. All the way back in the car, Agatha sobbed while Martin just stared morosely out of the window. I was too upset to cry.

Back in the orphanage, Sister Beatrice was almost gleeful at our failed attempt to run away.

'That's the devil in you,' she cackled triumphantly. 'The devil is in you, Irene Coogan, and he makes you do wicked things!'

And with that she whacked me across the back of the head so hard my teeth clanged together and my head rang.

'You're to go see the Mother Superior straight away!'

Standing outside the Mother Superior's office, Agatha and I were both too terrified to speak. I'd seen the Mother Superior before but I'd never had anything to do with her. She was a tall, well-built nun in her mid-fifties and when she opened the door her expression was so severe I nearly wet myself.

'Just you first.' She pointed a thin, bony finger at me and Agatha shrank back on the wooden bench while I followed her reluctantly, my knees shaking with fear.

'How dare you,' she started quietly once I was inside her small, sparsely decorated office. I looked around – just a crucifix on one wall and a picture of Christ on another.

There was a desk, chair and filing cabinet in the corner – that was it. The Mother Superior leaned on her desk, fingers white where they bent at the knuckles. Her voice soon rose to a bellow:

'HOW DARE YOU! Taking the nuns' kindness and mercy and throwing it back in their faces like the horrible, ungrateful child that you are.'

Martin had been ordered back to the nursery – they must have assumed we had forced him to go with us. I kept my eyes fixed on the floor, just praying for it all to be over quickly.

'You! Irene. You are a very wicked little girl. A bad girl from a bad family and what you did today, well, it doesn't surprise me. There is evil in a child that runs away from goodness. Now you'll have the evil beaten out of you. Bend over.'

I bent over the desk as she took off a thick leather belt. I tried to brace myself for what was to come next but nothing could have prepared me for the pain.

Whoomph! The force of the belt threw me forward and into the desk, knocking the wind out of me. Pain erupted through my body – Jesus, it was unbearable! The worst thing I'd ever felt in my life. Tears sprang immediately to my eyes and even as she struck the second and the third blows across my bottom, I sobbed like a baby. Big, snotty, gulping sobs as she walloped me again and again.

As soon as it was over she ordered me back to class and

I ran down the corridor as fast as I could, not even looking back to catch my sister Agatha's eye. I hoped it wouldn't be as bad for her. The rest of the day I perched delicately on the edge of my seat as I couldn't sit down properly for the pain.

I didn't see Agatha until it was time for bed. I kept trying to catch her eye but she wouldn't look at me. I could tell from the way she was moving that she was in pain too. That night, after lights out, I listened as my sister wept quietly to herself.

'Aggie!' I whispered. 'Aggie! Are you okay?'

Silence.

'Did you get a beating, Aggie?'

From under the covers came a tiny little whimper: 'We didn't get to see Mammy.'

And then the crying started up again.

'I know,' I said sorrowfully. I was sad too. 'Aggie, you're not angry with me are you?'

'What for?'

'You know, for the running away.'

'No, no, I'm not angry, Irene,' she said. Then she sighed and we both stopped talking. There was nothing more to say.

From then on, I decided, I'd try to keep my head down and stay out of trouble. But at school the next day Mrs Lawley was in a foul mood. She stomped around the classroom, swiping at us for doing the tiniest little thing wrong. Half-way through the morning I jumped when I heard her call out: 'Irene Coogan! Come to the front!'

Nervously, I walked to the front of the class – all around me the rest of the class scribbled furiously at their desks. Nobody looked up or caught my eye. They were all just relieved it wasn't them. *Oh God, what have I done now?* I wondered. My backside was already killing me from the beating with the belt. Now I expected to get my hands blistered again. I stood in front of the desk and held out my hands.

'No, come round here,' Mrs Lawley insisted, indicating that I should come behind the desk to where she was sitting. Confused, I did as I was told. Once I was close enough, she grabbed my hand and put it under her skirt and between her legs. She wasn't wearing any knickers and I felt her . . . her . . . *urgh!*

I recoiled in shock and dragged my hand away. *What is going on now? This isn't right! You have to wear your knickers – that's what we are always told, or it is sinful.* My mind raced and my stomach flipped over. Mrs Lawley grabbed my hand again and, with a quick glance across the classroom, making sure the others had their heads down, she put my hand right back there. Now I started to cry. This was too much. I didn't like it.

I pulled my hand away again and whimpered, 'No, I don't want to do it. I don't want to do it.'

She grabbed my wrist now and held on hard as she pushed my hand down between her legs, but I was crying loudly and a few curious heads bobbed up. She let go and I pulled my hands up to my chest.

'Get back to your work!' she shouted at the children. Eventually, frustrated with my refusal to do what she wanted, she picked up her ruler. Relief flooded through me when I saw she only planned to hit me now.

'Hands out,' she snapped. 'Back of the hands facing up.'

Getting the ruler on the back of my hands was even more painful than the palms. But it was better than that other thing she'd tried to make me do.

I no longer prayed for my mammy to come and get me – I knew that she wasn't coming. So each morning when I opened my eyes and saw I was still in my small, cold bed in St Grace's, a heavy sadness settled on my chest like a thick blanket. It became harder and harder to drag myself around, I felt so sad. I tried to talk to Agatha but she didn't want to know. She had stopped trusting me after our escape plan had gone wrong. As for Mrs Lawley, I didn't talk to anyone else about what had happened. Who could I tell? There was nobody in here who was kind to us children. It felt like we were always in the wrong, no matter what we did or didn't do. To the nuns and the staff, it seemed that just the fact of us being here meant we were bad children.

As the weeks wore on, I saw that Mrs Lawley did that dirty thing with other girls too. She got other children to go up to the front and stand behind the desk to make them 'touch her'. It was horrible but, like everyone else, I kept my head down and pretended I couldn't see what she was doing. We didn't want to get into trouble and we didn't want to embarrass the girl in the front of the class either. She tried it a few more times with me but each time I struggled and each time I got the ruler. That *thing* – it scared me. It was different from the beatings, I knew that. I knew you weren't meant to do stuff like that. I mean, even touching yourself was banned. A child could be beaten half to death for such a thing. We girls weren't even allowed to hold hands with each other because the nuns said it was dirty, something I really couldn't understand because it was just holding hands with another girl. But this? This was disgusting! So each time, I resisted. I struggled and cried and made too much fuss and eventually she gave up and just beat me with the ruler.

But as bad as it was in school, it was still a million times better than going to the nursery. I hated it in there, I hated all the crying babies and the staff who made it so much worse. Each day I dreaded leaving school at 2.30 p.m. to go to the nursery. My duties were usually the same – changing the nappies and the beds, changing the sheets, scrubbing the floors and helping the older ones with the potties. They had a terrible time, the toddlers, when they were learning to go on the potty. The nuns would strap them down for hours at a time. At night I lay awake, thinking of all those babies and their mammies and daddies, thinking about whether they knew their poor babies were being tortured, day in, day out. If they knew, they wouldn't leave them there, I reasoned. If they knew, they would take them away from that place. It tormented me, worrying about those children all the time.

One day I was instructed to go to the infirmary where they had a clothing supplies cupboard. A two-year-old girl needed new shoes. When I got there I told the sister in charge the reason for my errand and she ordered me to wait in the corridor while she fetched a pair of shoes that were the right size. Out in the corridor, I leaned against the wall and looked around. It was light here thanks to large windows along the top of the green walls and polished wooden floors. I wondered who had polished those floors this morning. My eyes roamed over the skirting and it was then I saw the socket. At that moment, my mother's voice popped into my head: 'Don't put your fingers in the socket. It's dangerous.'

It was like something clicked in my head. The socket was dangerous! This was my chance – my way out. Until this moment I hadn't thought of harming myself. It just never occurred to me. But now I could see a way for me to escape my painful existence. I didn't want to be around any more; life was too horrible and scary all the time. I went to sleep frightened, I woke up frightened. It seemed like there was no escape from the fear and the pain – until now. The white socket seemed to grow as I moved towards it. I couldn't stop myself – I felt my hand being drawn towards it like a magnet and before I knew what I was doing I had stuck my little fingers fully inside. Instantaneously, I felt a powerful surge through my body and I flew across the room . . .

Then I woke up. For a while my vision was blurry and my head pounded. I felt groggy and disorientated. *Where am I? What happened?* A fuzzy outline sharpened up to reveal a man in a white coat sitting at the edge of my bed and a nun standing behind him. Everything was white – was I in heaven? The man took hold of my wrist and turned it over, then he counted as he looked at the clock on the wall. After that, he shone a little torch in my eyes. *No, this isn't heaven. I must be in the infirmary.* Suddenly it all came flooding back. The socket, the electric surge. I must have passed out. A deep sadness swelled in my chest – it hadn't worked! I was still here.

The man, I realized, must be a doctor. He put away his little torch, sighed, folded his hands on his lap and looked at me with distaste.

'Why did you do a stupid thing like that?' he said. 'That was dangerous.'

I felt a lump in my throat and the tears threatened to fall but I didn't want to cry in front of him and I wanted him to know the truth.

'It's because they're hurting me,' I said, unable to meet

his eye. 'They're doing things to me here. And I don't like it.'

'What do you mean?'

'In the nursery.'

I paused. *How much should I tell him?* I felt dirty even talking about it but I knew I had to tell the truth. He was a doctor! Doctors were meant to make people better. Maybe if I told him, he could make the nuns stop.

'They're . . . putting things into us.' I gasped even as I spoke and the tears spilled out. A second later, I crumpled in distress. I had said it. I had done it!

'I told you, doctor,' I heard the nun say somewhere above my head. 'Evil. She's a very evil child. The devil's in her.'

I looked up beseechingly then. *Won't you help me, doctor? Won't anyone help me?* But the doctor seemed disappointed. By now the nun had wandered off and he got up off my bed, shook his head and followed her out.

I lay there, horrified. *He's not going to help me. This is it now, this is my life. I'm stuck here and there's nothing I can do to escape – I couldn't run away and I couldn't hurt myself. Nothing is going to get better, nobody is coming to rescue me so I better just get used to it.*

Something inside me seemed to disappear then. I don't know what it was or how it happened but it felt like I went away inside myself and some other little girl came and took over from her. And this little girl had just one thought on her mind – survival. That night, as I lay in the infirmary re-covering, I told myself that I would just have to get on with it. Head down, mouth shut. Just get through it. *You're on your own now, Irene, so don't expect help from anyone.*

The next day I was pronounced well enough to return to the dorm but, strangely enough, instead of being sent to the nursery after school I was put to making rosary beads instead. There were about thirty of us in a large room and we were given the wire and the beads and we had to make them a certain way, the whole thing from beginning to end. The wire was sharp, and by the end of the first day it felt like my fingers were torn to ribbons. Still, at least it was better than being in the nursery.

We had to make at least twelve a week and I made sure I just kept my head down and got on with my work. I shut myself away in my own little world and tried to concentrate on staying out of trouble. At least with the rosary beads I wasn't tortured by seeing all the little babies and what the nuns and Bernie did to them. Still, at night, in the silence, I could hear the sound of the babies crying. They sounded so real but we were too far away from the nursery ward to hear them so they must have been in my head.

I got used to the random beatings – no matter how much I tried to be good, it was impossible to avoid getting a daily wallop across the head. I could be hit if I was talking in line, if my hemline was down, my hair was too messy, my shoes were dirty, I didn't clear up my bed properly, I gave the nuns cheek, I didn't move quickly enough, I moved too quickly, I prayed too loudly, I didn't pray enough, if I was late or early . . . on and on it went. The list was endless and made no sense. I could never get it all right so I just got used to getting hit. The beatings only served to fill a deep well of injustice inside me. Apart from that, life was more or less a daily struggle to get enough food in my stomach so that I didn't keel over.

As for my brother and sisters, it was hard to think about them. I didn't talk to anyone; I was just trying to get through it without anyone really noticing me. Agatha would take herself off to the nursery in the evenings to see Cecily and Martin because she was like a mammy to them, but I didn't go. Not after what happened to me while I was there. Something inside me had gone away and I didn't know if it was ever coming back.

At Christmas we put on a Nativity show. We did our little show in the church on Christmas Eve and the place was packed with ordinary people from the town. For the first time I realized that the nuns acted differently when there were outsiders around. They put on their best voices and they didn't shout at us or beat us in front of the visitors. I was given the role of King Herod. We had had rehearsals but they were a chore and I didn't enjoy them at all. Now in the church I nearly forgot my lines because I was too busy scanning the faces of the women in the audience, looking for my mother, but she hadn't come.

Afterwards the Mother Superior gave a speech about

how they were grateful to all the outsiders and their donations to the orphanage. Then, incredibly, one of the visitors was invited onto the stage and he handed out a box of chocolates to every child in the Nativity play. My eyes nearly popped out of my head when I was given a gorgeous box with a big gold bow – Butlers Chocolates! Oh my God, I'd never had one Butlers chocolate before, let alone a whole boxful!

One by one we filed out of the church and back towards our dorms. I held my box of chocolates in front of me like one of the Kings holding his precious offering to the Baby Jesus. But this was better than gold, frankincense or myrrh – this was chocolate! Each child who carried a box of chocolates was excited. *I'll share them with Agatha, Martin and Cecily*, I decided as I walked back. *Then we'll all get something special this Christmas.*

But the moment I stepped back inside the orphanage, Sister Beatrice, who was standing in the doorway, ripped my box out of my hands. I opened my mouth to object but Sister Beatrice barked at me, 'Keep walking, Irene. Come on – don't dawdle.'

More children were coming in behind me and all the ones with boxes of chocolates had them whipped off them. Some seemed resigned, like this was what they had expected, others were as shocked and outraged as I was. They had given the chocolates to us but then, when the outsiders weren't looking, the nuns had taken them away!

Nobody knew the truth about these cruel nuns because they never let the outsiders see what was really going on. I didn't get anything for Christmas that year and I wondered for a long time who ate my chocolates.

By January, we had been in St Grace's for three months and I was used to the daily rituals. At the end of each week we were made to stand in a line to hold out our knickers for the Mother Superior to inspect, just to make sure we hadn't soiled ourselves. I dreaded these inspections – they were humiliating and horrible for everyone. I was always terrified they would pick me and put my knickers on the pole like in the first week, so sometimes I tried to clean my knickers during the week under the tap in the sink. It wasn't easy and since we only had one pair at a time I had to put them back on wet, but it was the only way. My heart skipped a beat every time the Mother Superior walked past. But then, when someone else was picked, that was awful too. Often the girl was beaten for being 'dirty' and then she had to stand at the window with the offending knickers on the pole. Of course, I was grateful it wasn't me but I always felt terrible for the girl who had to stand there at the window. It was painful for all of us to watch.

That month the nuns cut my hair. I had long brown hair which was nearly halfway down my back when I was ordered to have a haircut.

'Please don't make it short,' I begged the older nun who

wielded the scissors. But she didn't take any notice. She cut it all off so that I was left with a very severe bob that just reached the bottom of my ears. I left the nun's room that day, my face burning with anger and outrage. My hair was my crowning glory! That was what my mother always said, that was what she told us. Our hair was our crowning glory and that's why we had to look after it and keep it long. That's what girls do! I'd been shorn like a sheep. I felt like I had nothing left that was mine any more. They just did what they liked with us and they never cared how we felt.

A few days later I was called up to the front of the class. I hated Mrs Lawley now – I hated her more than I hated anybody in my life before. She was a mean, wicked old witch. I didn't even learn anything in her classes – it was all just copying her writing and keeping my head down so I didn't get the ruler. Recently she had also started to use the cane on us.

Since St Grace's orphanage school was the only one in the area, it took a lot of children from the tenement blocks too. But one thing I had noticed was that Mrs Lawley never did that dirty thing with the children who had mammies and daddies to go home to each night. These girls didn't get beaten like the rest of us, or made to do horrible things, it was only us orphanage children. Today she wanted me to do *that thing* to her but I shouted 'No!' and struggled so much that this time she brought out the cane and she beat me really hard on my hands. Then she beat me on the back of the legs as well. I hobbled back to my desk and eased myself down gingerly on my seat. The bloody cow! I hated her so much I wished she would die.

It took me longer than normal to get to church for prayers that lunchtime and so I got another beating in the dining hall for being late. After lunch I didn't even bother to go into the yard to get some bread – I was in too much pain and I knew I wouldn't be quick enough today. Instead I turned up towards the school and limped into the class-room early, just to give myself enough time to sit down. Ouch! My legs and hands throbbed continuously. I felt sick from the pain.

I clutched the edge of Mrs Lawley's desk as I waddled up towards the end of the classroom where I usually sat, and just as I was moving off my eye landed on the cane. Without even thinking about what I was doing, I picked it up and held it by each end. Then I pushed it hard across my knee until it snapped in two. As I held each splintered end a tiny smile of triumph broke out on my face. *Ha! Now you won't be able to beat any more children today at least.*

Well, I was wrong about that. When she got back in the class Mrs Lawley went mad and demanded to know who had broken her cane.

'I done it!' I shouted defiantly from the back of the class-room. I felt brave as I shouted at her, 'I done it because you hurt me!'

She beat me then with half a cane. It's funny though – it

didn't hurt half as much as I expected it would. Though my behind was sore and numb, some part of me was still happy that I broke the cane.

9

IRENE
⊤

Dad

My heart pounded as I ran towards the small visitors' building. I was excited and nervous all at the same time. *My father is here!* The words chased themselves around my head over and over again but still I couldn't quite catch a hold of their meaning. My father? I didn't know my father!

It was a breezy Saturday afternoon in March and the nun who had come to fetch me from my work had announced it so casually that it didn't seem real.

'Irene Coogan to the visitors' room, please,' she called out across the rows of children threading rosary beads. 'Your father and your grandmother have come to see you.'

For a moment I had stayed completely still in my seat, afraid to move in case she had got it wrong. *Did she really mean my father?* I'd never even met my father before; at least,

I couldn't remember meeting him. He'd always been away in England working. *Is he really here? Now?*

I walked into the small building and saw immediately to my right there was a spacious sitting room with green sofas arranged around small wooden tables. This was where the other children had their family visits but I'd never been here before now. Sitting in one corner was my grandmother – my father's mother, who had brought up Aidan and who I recognized and had seen a few times before – next to a man with jet-black hair in a snow-white shirt. As I crept in nervously, the man rose to his feet. Goodness me! He was such a tall, handsome man – a firm, square jaw, pale blue eyes and a long straight nose. He was just like how I imagined my fantasy father looked. Was this really my father? Shyly, I went towards the two of them and my grandmother exclaimed, 'Irene! Come here, child – don't lurk in the doorway like that. Come on!'

I sidled up to them and mumbled 'hello.' My father smiled back.

'Look at you, Irene!' he said. 'You're a proper little girl now, aren't you?'

I didn't know how to reply so I just sat down next to them. I played with the hem of my corduroy skirt as I snatched sidelong glances at my father, still in awe at his movie-star good looks. He was like no man I'd seen before.

'Don't slouch, child,' my grandmother chided, before

handing me an apple. I took it gratefully. It was rare to get fruit in St Grace's.

Before long Agatha ran in, shouting, 'Daddy! Daddy!'

Our father jumped to his feet then and held out his arms. Agatha dived straight into them and he swung her round in an affectionate hug. Agatha was four years older than me so she had seen our father lots of times before. Martin and Cecily came in next and Daddy's eyes lit up when he saw Cecily. He barely even noticed Martin, he was so smitten with my baby sister.

Each of us got an apple and Agatha asked Daddy lots of questions about England, Mammy, Peter and Frances.

'Are you going to take us out of here?' she asked hopefully.

'No, I can't do that,' he said. 'Your mother is still in the convalescent home. She's not very well. But I'm coming in two weeks for your communion, Irene.'

I should have been pleased but I was struck by sadness and, a second later, began to cry. My father exchanged a worried look with my grandmother, who prodded me and asked: 'What are you crying for?'

'They're hurting us here,' I told her. 'They beat us all the time and they hurt the little ones. I don't want to stay here any more.'

Thwack! The slap came so suddenly and out of the blue, I was temporarily shocked out of crying. My grandmother had hit me across the face. Instinctively my hand went to my stinging cheek.

'You're a liar!' she hissed at me. 'The nuns don't do them things and you know it. How dare you say things like that about these nuns that are taking care of you and feeding you!'

'It's true,' I whimpered.

'No, it's NOT true, you evil child, and this is the place to sort you out!'

I felt humiliated in front of my father but also defeated by the force of my grandmother's response. None of my siblings said anything – even though they all knew what I said was the truth. So I didn't say another word and half an hour later it was time for them to go. It had been a strange and difficult encounter. In the six months I'd been at St Grace's I'd not had one visitor and seeing my grandmother, and my father for the first time, had been so thrilling. But the reality of seeing them sitting there, knowing they were going to walk out of the orphanage without us, had made me angry. Why couldn't they take us away? Why did we all have to stay here? I didn't understand it at all.

Just two weeks later and I was about to see my father again. It was the day of my communion, a very important day for any seven-year-old girl. To mark the occasion, all us girls who were taking communion were allowed to stay overnight with our families. Since Mammy was in the convalescent home, that meant my grandmother's home. For the children who had no mammies or daddies, strangers offered to take them out. That morning, instead of putting on my usual dark green skirt, I eased my arms into the pure white communion dress I'd been given for the day.

'Oh, you look so beautiful!' Agatha breathed appreciatively as I spun round in the lovely cotton dress with lacy bits on the sleeves. I even had a pearly tiara for my hair. When I put it on I felt like a real princess.

'Smell that!' I exclaimed, smiling at my sister. Today the nuns laid on a proper cooked breakfast for the children taking communion to share with their parents, and the air was thick with the sweet, heady scent of frying bacon. My stomach groaned in anticipation but I wanted to be careful with my dress so I moved slowly as I went downstairs. My daddy was already in the dining room, tucking into a large plate piled high with bacon, eggs, sausage and toast. I broke into a grin the moment I saw him and he nodded back.

'Lovely dress!' he said, pointing at the layers of lace at my hem with his fork. 'Come on, get some grub down you. Big day today!'

I sat down next to him and he put some egg, sausage and bacon on my plate then carried on eating. For a moment I hesitated – my hands were shaking with nerves. What if I dropped something on my dress and ruined it? I was desperate to eat something but I couldn't trust myself.

'I wouldn't mind living here mesel' if you get fed like this every day!' Daddy smiled gratefully through a mouthful of sausage.

'We don't usually get a cooked breakfast,' I said quietly. 'Mainly, it's just porridge.'

'What?' Daddy turned to me but I didn't want to upset him so I just shook my head and sat there with my hands in my lap. After he'd finished everything on his plate, Daddy looked around him, satisfied. Then he noticed the untouched food on my plate.

'Well, I'm not going to let that go to waste,' he said as he swapped our plates over, and in another minute my food was gone.

'The body of Christ.' I opened my mouth to receive the little wafer from the priest. I sucked on it carefully as I had seen all the others do until it was soft enough to slip down my throat. We had gone straight from breakfast to the church in the orphanage and now I was at the altar making my first communion with half a dozen other girls.

'The blood of Christ,' the priest intoned solemnly and offered me the chalice. I took a little sip and the strange sweet liquid burned my throat. An hour later and I was back outside in the open air, grinning from ear to ear.

All the other children crowded around us, admiring our white dresses and congratulating us. Once again, I felt so special, like a princess. I knew this wasn't my dress and I would have to give it back tomorrow but, just for today,

I could pretend it was mine. And then my father said the words I'd been longing to hear.

'Alright, Irene.' He took my hand. 'Let's get out of here.'

I practically skipped by his side that day as we walked out of the gates of St Grace's – it was a gorgeous, warm spring day and my heart swelled in my chest.

'Where are we going?' I asked him.

'To see your mother,' he replied. 'She'd never forgive me if she didn't get a look at you in your communion dress.'

We caught a bus from the main road that took us to a large building in the middle of town. Once inside, we were directed towards a stuffy sitting room where lots of old ladies sat in large armchairs with rugs on their knees. In one corner I spotted my mother in a dressing gown with a rug across her lap and my sister Frances by her side.

'Oh, look at you!' Frances exclaimed the moment she laid eyes on me. Right then, I wanted to cry. I was so full of emotion. She jumped up and enveloped me in a big hug but Mammy didn't move.

'You look gorgeous,' Frances whispered and gave me a little wink. Mammy smiled and nodded and then she turned to Frances. 'Will you get me a cup of tea, Fran love?'

I sat next to her for the next twenty minutes while she spoke to my father about her recovery. Nobody spoke to me – she didn't even ask about the others in St Grace's. Instead, Daddy loudly announced to everyone in the room that I had just made my communion and a few old ladies offered coins to put in my communion bag.

Before I knew it we were outside again and I was running to keep up with my father.

'Will my mother be well again soon?' I asked him as we turned a corner.

'Ah, who knows?' he replied tetchily. 'It's up to her. Sometimes I reckon she prefers it in there anyways.'

I tried to make sense of this as Daddy led us down a wide, busy road. We crossed over and then turned down a small side street – halfway down we stopped at a pub.

'Billy!' Daddy greeted the barman jovially. 'Get us a pint, would you? My little girl here just made her first communion.'

All day long we stayed in that pub. Every time someone new came in, Daddy called out to them about my communion and they held out a coin for my bag. Steadily, it filled up until it was heavy with money. Daddy drank pint after pint while I sat on the bench next to him, fiddling with my bag and admiring the coins. Every now and then Daddy got me a glass of water but no food. Just as the sun was casting long shadows outside and an orange glow settled on the buildings, Daddy looked up to the clock on the wall.

'It's six, Irene. S'teatime,' he slurred, his head bobbing back and forward. 'Better get back to your granny's place.'

I hadn't eaten all day so I was more than ready to leave

– it had been a long day and my bum had gone numb from sitting on a hard bench for hours.

Daddy staggered and weaved us through the back streets until we reached my grandmother's house. She met us at the front door with a sour expression and ushered us inside. She sat me down at the table in the kitchen and put a boiled egg and a slice of toast in front of me, which I attacked with gusto. While I was eating, Daddy and Granny shared a pot of tea. As they talked, Daddy took hold of the communion bag laid on the table next to me. He didn't even look in my direction as he poured out the coins onto the table and then deftly divided them into two piles. He pushed one pile towards my grandmother, who scooped up the coins and deposited them in the pocket of her apron. The other he put in his own pocket. Then he dropped two pennies back into my bag and pushed it across the table towards me. By then, I was so tired I didn't care. An hour later my grandmother led me upstairs to a small bedroom where she stripped off my dress and put me to bed in my vest and knickers. Almost immediately I fell fast asleep.

Waking up the next day was strange. I lay there for a while listening to the unfamiliar sounds of my granny's house: gurgling pipes, creaking floorboards, neighbours greeting each other in the street and cars revving their engines. It was lovely to be out of the dorm and away from the nuns for a night.

After a while I got up and put my communion dress

back on – I didn't have anything else to wear. When I crept downstairs, Granny was at the stove, stirring a pan of porridge. I sat at the table and, in a little while, she put a lovely, steaming bowl in front of me. It was exactly the way porridge should be – creamy and sweet, cooked all the way through, not like the muck they gave us in St Grace's. I plucked up the courage to ask her if she could keep me at her house, just until Mammy recovered.

'You're going back to the nuns and that's final,' she answered firmly.

'Please, Granny, please don't send me back there . . .'

'That's enough!' she snapped. 'Now finish your porridge, quickly now, and get your shoes on. Your father can't wait around all day.'

No sooner had I finished than we said a hurried goodbye and I was ushered outside to her front porch. In another second, her door was shut.

Daddy and I got on the bus again, but he didn't seem in a very cheerful mood. In fact, he was grumpy for most of the way and if I asked him a question he just grunted at me. We got off the bus next to a parade of shops, and one was a sweet shop.

'Stop, Daddy!' I shouted. 'I want to get some toffees!'

I had two pennies left in my communion bag and I knew I wouldn't have another chance to buy something. So Daddy took me into the sweet shop and I chose a bag of toffees. Carefully, I hid them inside my communion bag. I had to get them inside St Grace's somehow so I could share them with Martin and Agatha. If the nuns found them they would take them off me for sure.

We approached the large gates of the orphanage. With every step up the driveway, I felt more and more miserable but Daddy didn't seem to notice. I wanted to stop next to the horse but he urged me on, telling me not to dawdle. There, at the front of the main building, the Mother Superior waited for us.

Her mouth was smiling but her eyes were cold.

'Irene. Mr Coogan.' She nodded politely.

'Sister.' Daddy nodded in response then he patted me on the back. 'Okay, in you go.'

I turned round to give him a hug but there was nobody there. He had already started back down the drive. I stood there for a while, watching his disappearing figure, hoping he would turn to wave. No. Nothing.

Now the Mother Superior dropped the fake smile and she looked me over distastefully. Finally she lost her patience.

'Do stop mooning around, Irene!' she exploded. 'He's gone. Now get inside!'

10

IRENE

A Failed Fostering

'Ah, Irene!' The Mother Superior welcomed me into her office with that special smile she put on for outsiders. Until this moment I had been nervous about being sent to the Mother Superior's office. *What have I done?* I thought as I scuttled up the corridor towards her room. I hadn't been told off for doing anything bad today so maybe it was something I hadn't noticed. My mind ran through the possibilities – was it something to do with my clothes? Or talking in church? Maybe I hadn't made my bed properly? I couldn't think of anything specific so I was full of dread as I approached her office and knocked on the door. But as soon as the Mother Superior flung the door open with that over-bearing, fake grin, I knew I wasn't there for a punishment.

There, in the room in front of me, sat a very well-dressed

man and woman. The lady wore a fawn-coloured stole around her neck and lots of make-up. The gentleman was in a smart dark suit and held a charcoal trilby at his knees. They weren't like anyone I'd met before – they were so well-to-do it made me feel uncomfortable. They both smiled at me anxiously.

'Irene, please.' The Mother Superior directed me to stand next to her desk while she sat down. 'Now, this is Mr and Mrs Donavan.' She indicated the woman and the man and they smiled at me again, even bigger smiles this time. I shifted nervously from one foot to another.

She went on, 'Mr and Mrs Donavan are going to take you home to live with them for a while.'

'What?' I exclaimed. I was too shocked for manners. 'What do you mean, Mother Superior?'

'I mean, Irene, they are going to give you a good home while we wait for your mother to get better, which may or may not happen.' She nodded at the couple again. They looked at me hopefully – the woman really was very lovely. She had beautiful blonde curls around her face and a string of pearls at her neck.

'We live in a nice house, Irene, with a garden and a dog,' the woman said to me now. She had a very posh voice, very polished. On her lap was a pair of neatly folded cream leather gloves.

'Do you like dogs, Irene?' she asked sweetly. I only remembered one dog in my life – a big black dog we once had called Jenny who barked whenever she saw a priest or a nun. Jenny didn't like the clergy – I didn't understand it at the time, in fact we all found it funny the way she went berserk whenever she saw a nun's habit. It drove Mammy mad because she loved nuns and it made her so embarrassed. The dog disappeared shortly after I turned four.

'Would you like a sweet, Irene?' The man's voice snapped me back to the present. He held out a striped paper bag of toffees towards me.

I froze. I couldn't make sense of any of it. *Who are these people? What do they want?* The seconds stretched out between us and silence filled the room.

'Well?' the Mother Superior sighed, exasperated. 'Aren't you going to take a toffee?'

'NO!' I shouted. Now the words came tumbling out of me: 'I don't want a sweetie and I don't want to go home with yous. I've got a mammy and a daddy. They're going to come and get me soon and I'll go home with them.'

None of this felt right. I just didn't understand why they wanted to take me home with them and I was frightened of this couple, especially the man, but I didn't know why.

'Irene, don't be such an ungrateful child,' the Mother Superior fumed. 'These good, kind people are offering to give you a home. You do want a nice home, don't you?'

'But I've got a home!' I wailed, tears springing to my eyes. 'I don't want to go with them. I don't know them. My brother and my sisters are here – I want to stay here with Agatha and Martin and Cecily.'

I was scared – even though I barely spoke to my sisters and brother these days, they were my family, the only family I had around me, and I loved them. This couple were strange, they were formal and frightening to me. The whole thing was too much. If these people took me away today I'd never get back to Mammy!

The couple turned to each other, dismayed. I could see they were upset but I didn't care. I didn't understand why the Mother Superior was trying to make me go home with these strangers when I already had a family of my own. The more the Mother Superior tried to insist I leave with Mr and Mrs Donavan, the harder I wept until, after a few minutes, I was nearly hysterical.

At that point, Mr Donavan interrupted. 'Sister, I think you better let her go back to her siblings. We don't want to distress the child any further.'

'Of course, Mr Donavan,' Mother Superior said through gritted teeth. 'Go on, Irene. Run along now!'

And with that I bolted out of the office and fled into the sitting room, cramming myself under one of the chairs. I knew I was in trouble and I didn't want sister to find me. After a few minutes I heard Mr and Mrs Donavan leaving under a siege of apologies from the Mother Superior. I listened as their footsteps disappeared down the corridor and, another minute later, heard the inevitable, 'IRENE COOGAN!'

Oh no! I gulped hard then slunk out from my hiding place. She stood in the doorway of the sitting room, her face purple with rage.

'MY OFFICE!' she thundered. 'NOW!'

I knew what was coming. Of course she would beat me for being so insolent and for not doing what she wanted but I didn't have any regrets. I had a mammy and a daddy and I knew one day I would go home to them.

'You're an evil child,' she insisted in tense, clipped tones as she closed the door behind us, then she hitched up her habit to unbuckle the thick leather belt that was fastened round her waist.

'A horrible, ungrateful child,' she went on. 'Nobody will ever love you, nobody will want you. You had your chance at a home and you threw it away! This is how you repay us and all we've done for you? BEND OVER!'

Later that night, once lights were out, I told Agatha all about what had happened.

She listened in horrified fascination as I described the Donavans, their fine clothes and eager expressions.

'But we've got a mammy and a daddy,' I explained in hushed tones. 'So I said no, I wouldn't go with them and the Mother Superior got really angry and that's when she beat me.'

'Why do you think they came to take *you* away?' Agatha asked, bemused. 'I mean, why you? There's lots of children here.'

'I don't know,' I murmured. 'It wasn't right. I didn't like the man.'

I lay awake that night, staring at the cracks in the ceiling, my legs and bottom blistered, red raw and pulsing with pain. It had all been so strange. All these years I had dreamed of another family, of a 'real' mammy and daddy who would one day take me away to live with them. Yet when some actual living, breathing people had come for me, I had found it so frightening. I realized it wasn't what I wanted after all. However hurtful she could be, I just wanted to be with my real mammy.

That Saturday I went into the dark space of the confessional box and for the first time in months I actually had something to say. Usually, I had to rack my brain to think of a 'confession' because, in truth, I never did anything wrong in St Grace's. What could I do? I had no freedom, no life, nothing beyond school, work and praying. But we didn't have a choice – we had to take confession every week, even if we hadn't done anything wrong. Some weeks I made stuff up, which I knew was a sin, and so the following week I could at least confess to telling a fib.

'Bless me, father, for I have sinned,' I whispered. 'It's been a week since my last confession. This week I shouted at some people and I went against the Mother Superior's wishes and I made her very cross at me.'

The father gave me absolution and told me to say ten Hail Marys and a decade of the rosary, just like he had the week before.

Strangely enough I did actually see my mother three weeks later, although she didn't see me. It was the last weekend in May and we were taken out of the orphanage for the annual show at the Jacob's biscuit factory. It was a special day of the year and most of the families from our council estate on the Liffey went along because there was free music and sweets.

At the orphanage, all the older children piled onto a bus for the drive to Bishop Street for the celebration and, for a very short time, as we sat on the upper deck, we could all pretend we were normal children. The buzz and the excitement in the air was wonderful. I stared out of the window the whole way, thrilled to get a glimpse at the outside world again. It had been over a month since my communion in April when I had left the orphanage with my father.

Suddenly my heart stopped. There, in the street directly below us, I saw my mother walking arm in arm with a friend, looking for all the world like a carefree young woman.

'Mammy!' I screamed and banged on the window. She

was talking and laughing with her friend, throwing her head back so her beautiful blonde locks tumbled down her back. She looked very much recovered to me, tottering down the street in her high heels and a tiny red skirt.

'Mammy!' I shouted desperately, banging away like crazy. 'Mammy! Look up! Look up!' But the bus rolled on and she never saw or heard me.

It was hard to enjoy the concert after that. I wanted to feel pleased that I'd seen her, but the way she had trotted along, smiling and giggling like a young girl, depressed me. I didn't want to admit to myself what had seemed so clear in those snatched few seconds. *She's happier without us. She doesn't miss us at all.*

For a couple of hours, we were paraded in front of the city, the 'poor, orphanage children', and everyone felt sorry for us and then we were sent back to hell. On the bus on the way back, my anger and despondency grew. Mammy didn't look ill to me and she was obviously out of the convalescent home, so why were we still living with the nuns? They didn't care about us. Nobody cared.

Life went on as usual in St Grace's – the nuns and staff scolded, slapped and beat us for no reason and then forced us to confess our sins. I struggled to get through each day and sank into oblivion each night. In St Grace's I had no dreams, just nightmares. It was the same for all of us. Often the night's silence was punctuated by the uneven, distressed cries of children fighting evil monsters in their sleep. Sometimes we woke up and the monsters were still there.

One Sunday in June, just after breakfast, we were instructed to line up in our year groups as it was a 'special day'.

'There are some volunteers coming today,' Sister Beatrice explained. 'Each couple has very generously offered to take a child out for the day. So look smart, behave, and – if you're lucky – they might pick you!'

A ripple of excitement passed down the line. We did our best to look nice for the visitors and, when they came, ten couples passed in front of all of us. I smiled winningly to try and look appealing. There was a young couple who stopped in front of me and after a whispered exchange the woman reached out and touched my arm.

'Hello – would you like to come and spend the day with us?' she asked. She had large hazel eyes and a sweet, earnest face.

'Yes please!' I responded eagerly.

Since there were only ten children for ten couples, we were allowed to have special clothes for the day. I was given a lovely dress with little daisies on it, a smart green coat with large black buttons and shiny brown patent shoes. Oh, the shoes! They were gorgeous and I couldn't stop looking at them as I was led to the visitors' building where the young couple waited for me.

'My name is Elizabeth,' the young woman introduced

herself. She couldn't have been more than twenty. 'But you can call me Betty. And this is my fiancé Mark.'

Mark nodded at me – he was short but very handsome with a clear, open expression. I don't know why but I liked and trusted these people from the start.

They were so sweet and so kind and they took me first bowling and then back to Mark's mother's house. I couldn't believe it when we walked in – the dining table was groaning with food. There were sandwiches, cakes, buns, doughnuts and biscuits – everything you could possibly want. My eyes nearly popped out of my head. I'd never seen so much lovely food all in one place before.

Betty broke into a giggle when she saw my mouth hanging open in shock.

'It's for you, Irene,' she laughed. 'Go on – help yourself!'

I looked around me then, confused and upset. I felt too scared to take anything.

'What's wrong with her?' Mark's mother whispered to him. 'Why won't she eat?'

'Ah, she's probably just a little overwhelmed, Mammy,' he reassured her. 'Give her a bit of time.'

The truth was I couldn't bring myself to touch any of that delicious food because I didn't feel I deserved any of it. I was a horrible, nasty, evil child. That's what the nuns had told me all this time and now I believed them. Kindness? I couldn't understand kindness. Eventually, Betty cajoled me into eating two egg and cress sandwiches and a slice of

Victoria sponge. It was heavenly – the nicest food I'd ever, ever tasted. Betty was so lovely – she told me all about her job as a clerical assistant and the wedding that she and Mark were planning. They were such warm and loving people, I wanted to stay in that house as long as possible. But, too soon, it was time to go back to the orphanage.

Despite Betty's bright and cheerful comments, I couldn't talk on the bus journey back to the orphanage. A huge lump stuck in my throat and a black mood settled over me as soon as we passed through the gates and up the drive. Eventually, as we approached the front doors I turned to them both in desperation.

'Please, please don't make me go in there,' I pleaded, clinging onto Betty's sleeve for dear life. 'Please take me with you. I want to go with you!'

She was alarmed at my outburst and shook her head apologetically. 'We can't, Irene,' she said. 'I'm so sorry but we really can't take you home with us. You have to go back.'

'Please, please,' I implored, as tears started to form. 'They'll let you take me if you ask them. They will! They do that! You can take me home and they won't mind a bit.'

'No, no, we can't do that,' Betty insisted, her eyes misting over with tears of her own. 'Mark? Mark, tell her we can't take her. Oh Lord, Irene. I'm so sorry.'

I burst into tears then and buried my face in her coat. She held me to her and for a while I just stood there, weeping silently. She rubbed my back and then pulled me away, kneeling down so that we were eye to eye. Her mascara had run a little down her cheeks.

'You're such a dear girl, Irene, and if I had a home to give you I would give it to you tomorrow, but I don't,' she explained patiently. 'We're not marrying for another six months and who knows what will happen by then. Maybe your own mammy will be better and she'll fetch you home to live with her?'

I bit down hard on my lip and in a thin little voice I whispered, 'Do you think so?'

'Of course,' she smiled. Then she drew me to her in a warm embrace and for the first time in many months I felt comforted. And safe. I let the tears roll freely off my cheeks.

We exchanged tearful waves at the door and then they turned to walk back down the drive. I waved for a long time, until I heard a tetchy voice above me say, 'That's enough. Get inside!'

It was the Mother Superior – she must have seen and heard everything. The way I had screamed and cried not to be sent back. In a panic, I took off down the corridor, desperate to get away from her before she could tell me off for making a fuss.

The blood pounded in my ears as I ran at full pelt until an icy blast stopped me dead: 'IRENE COOGAN!'

Terrified, I turned round and there she was, at the end of the corridor, her face a mask of fury. In that moment, everything I'd eaten that day just fell out of me. I stood, helpless with fear, as my body collapsed in fright. The Mother Superior flew at me. The next thing, her hand made contact with my face and I rose up off the ground with the force and fell back down again in a crumpled heap. My nostrils filled with the scent of my own faeces and I saw my beautiful clothes were smeared and soiled.

'Look what you've done, you disgusting child!' she snorted with loathing. 'The devil is in you, Irene Coogan, and I'm going to make it my business to beat the devil out of you. Now get a bucket and clean up your revolting mess!'

I didn't get any tea that evening – I was too busy cleaning the corridor and myself. All the nice feelings I had from my day out were destroyed in an instant. I went to bed that night tired, hungry and ashamed.

In July the school holidays started and some of us younger children were shipped out by bus to a different orphanage in the beautiful countryside for three months. It was all open fields swaying with wheat and corn and long sunny days. Since there was no school we were allowed to play outside all day long, which was better than being stuck in a classroom with Mrs Lawley. Only two nuns from St Grace's came with us; the rest of the nuns were from the country and they didn't beat us, which was a nice change.

But while other children were happy to skip and play all day long, running around, chasing one another seemingly without a care in the world, I sat in a corner of the yard most of the time, just staring at them all. *How can they be so happy?* I wondered to myself. *What is there to laugh about?* I didn't feel anything any more – not happiness, not sadness. Nothing. I was empty.

Cecily and Martin were here too but I didn't have much to do with them. The older children like Agatha stayed behind in the orphanage.

One thing that was better about being on holiday in the country was the food – the vegetables were much fresher and now I could actually tell the difference between the vegetables in my stew. Cabbage, carrots, turnips, swedes and potatoes – I took real pleasure in identifying and savouring each mouthful.

Since the church was at the other end of the village, we were marched through every morning and evening for Mass and Benediction. From the orphanage we passed down the main street with all the shops and saw the grocers, butchers and bakery every day – there was a market there too so it was a busy little place with lots of people at the weekend. Clumping past the villagers in our big hobnailed boots and gabardine coats, I felt their eyes on me and I hated it. Sometimes I even heard them, heads cocked to one side, muttering to one another.

'Oh, look at the poor little orphanage children – here for their holidays.'

'Aren't they sweet?'

'Very well-behaved. There but for the grace of God . . .'

'Indeed. Indeed.'

I kept my head down as we went by, angry and resentful. I didn't want their pity. I hated being paraded in front of the villagers like this. It was almost a relief when summer ended and we could go back to St Grace's where we didn't have to face ordinary folks day in, day out, reminding us how different we were, reminding me daily of the rejection at the heart of my life.

Back at St Grace's, I stopped expecting things to get better and something in my heart hardened and closed up. The weeks passed slowly. I didn't cry any more when the nuns beat me, I didn't want to give them the satisfaction. I rarely saw Agatha because she had been moved into the older girls' dormitory, and I avoided going into the nursery so I didn't see much of Martin or Cecily. I didn't think about them either. I didn't think about anything. It was better not to think or hope or dream. It was less heartbreaking. So I became like a machine. The food went into my mouth now and I didn't even taste it. At night, I closed my eyes and, instead of dreaming of going home, I just fell straight to sleep, relieved that another day was over. So when the nun fetched me one brisk morning in November to tell me my mother had come to take me home, at first I didn't actually believe her.

11

IRENE

⊤

The Orphanages

I was beside myself with excitement by the time I raced into the sitting room of the visitors' building. There she stood, waiting for us all. She looked so pretty in a short, light blue mac and knee-high cream boots. Mammy! I ran up to her and hugged her round the waist. Cecily was already there, dressed in her coat, and soon Agatha and Martin joined us.

'Okay, okay,' Mammy tutted irritably. 'Let go of me now. Are we all ready to go home?'

'Yes!' I shouted. I couldn't get out of that place quick enough. It had been the longest and worst year of my life. I had all but given up hope of ever going home again, so to hear those words almost made me want to cry. All I wanted at that moment was to get as far away from these cruel and nasty nuns as possible.

On the bus on the way home, we all clamoured for

information. Did we live in the same house as before? Was Mammy all better? Where were Peter and Frances? What about Daddy? Mammy did her best to answer our questions.

'Your father is home for Christmas so they said you lot could all come out and then we'll see how it goes,' Mammy explained. 'We're still in the same house. I'm well enough for the minute but who knows how long that'll last? You'll all just have to be good and help me out as much as possible so that I can stay well enough to look after yous all. You're still enrolled in the school at St Grace's, mind, so you'll be going back there for your lessons and maybe if I need a rest, you might have to go back to the orphanage for a little while, but we'll see how it goes. Peter and Frances are back at home already.'

It was a strange homecoming, not at all how I'd imagined it. For one thing, the downstairs windows were all boarded up and there was barely a stick of furniture in the place. It wasn't at all homely. Mum said she'd had to sell all our furniture to help make ends meet and the boards had been put up to stop people breaking in while she was in the convalescent home. There was one settee still in the living room but it was falling apart so we sat on orange crates instead. There was no table, just one bed for us children in the front bedroom and another for Mammy and Daddy in their room. And that was it.

But the biggest shock of all was that our father was there. I'd never spent any time with my daddy before so it was very odd getting used to living with a grown man. At least it meant there was plenty of food that Christmas. It soon became clear to us all that Daddy loved his food and he insisted my mother cook a large turkey with all the trimmings and a cake. It was grand having home-cooked food again – I'd almost forgotten what real meat tasted like and the smell of my mother's apple pie filling the house was exquisite. Mind you, I couldn't eat all that much as my stomach wasn't used to rich food any more. I even got a present on Christmas Day! It was a doll – she had an arm and an eye missing and all her hair had been chopped off but I didn't care. She was my doll and, to me, she was the best thing in the world.

For the first couple of weeks, I loved just having my freedom back and I took myself off for hours at a time, wandering along the Liffey or through the barren, muddy fields. For the first time in a year, I felt I could breathe freely again. And I cherished being able to spend quiet time with my own thoughts. Though I was almost always lonely in the orphanage, I was rarely alone. I had missed solitude.

Even though I was still enrolled in school at St Grace's, being a 'day girl' was a whole different experience to living there. The teachers were nice to you because they knew you were going home to a mammy and daddy every night and of course we didn't have to live with the nuns. I was anxious to put my experiences at St Grace's behind me, as were my siblings. None of us talked about it to our parents or among ourselves. We just wanted to forget it ever happened.

It felt good to be back with my family but there were subtle changes that only revealed themselves slowly. For a start, Peter was different. He was nine years old and there was a simmering anger within him now that occasionally burst to the surface. While we had been housed in St Grace's he was taken in by the priests at a boys' Catholic home. It had changed him – he didn't talk to us easily any more and he seemed to loathe our father. The pair couldn't be in the same room for more than five minutes before a fight broke out, and then Daddy would beat him with his hands or take the belt to him. It wasn't the same with my mother – Peter adored my mother and she wouldn't hear a word against him. And sometimes that made things worse.

My mother and father weren't lovey-dovey like I'd seen other couples – they didn't hold hands or look at each other with fondness. They didn't even talk much. I knew they were married but the way they acted it was like they were just living in the same house. My mother put food in front of my father and barely looked at him. He ate his food then went out. The only time they said two words to each other was to argue. Occasionally Dad tried to make my mother have a Guinness with him and then she would be nice to him but the next day it seemed she was angrier than ever. But Daddy was always really happy. It was strange and confusing.

It was almost a relief when Daddy returned to his work as a truck driver in England after Christmas. The house was quieter, less of a battleground. We attended our school lessons in St Grace's and, for a while, things went back to the way they were before the orphanage. Mammy still had a hot temper and a vicious tongue but at least I didn't live under the tyranny of the nuns. There was only one of Mammy, but there were dozens of nuns! And even though the children on our estate teased us and called us 'The Orphanages', I didn't mind so much. I stood up for myself more and more – I fought back.

Now that Mammy was getting social welfare, there was enough money to feed us all so it was rare I went a day without food. In time, the boards came off the windows. But Mammy's health was up and down and she still took it into her head occasionally to sit us all down to watch her 'commit suicide' with her pills and a bottle of whisky. It meant we were sent back to St Grace's every few months to give her a 'rest'.

Things were starting to change a little at St Grace's too. There was a record player in the living room now and a couple of games as well. The cruelty was still there but the nuns didn't beat me as much – I didn't know if it was because I kept my head down and I knew how to stay out of trouble or because they knew we were going back home to our mammy. They were only short stays this time, the longest one being two months; even so, I was always scared I would get stuck there for good and Mammy wouldn't come and get me. One time they didn't have space for all of us and we were placed in another home called the Rose House.

The Rose House couldn't have been more different from St Grace's – for one thing it was run by kind, gentle nurses. There wasn't a nun in sight. The beds were soft and warm with crisp, white sheets, the food was tasty and wholesome, the sitting room was filled with toys and games and there was always fun going on. In the Rose House the children laughed and smiled – there was happiness in the air and that was because the nurses were nice people. They spoke in a soft, soothing way which made you feel they really cared. Nurse Abigail was my favourite – she was plump and cuddly and always gave me big hugs. If I was having a bad day or felt sad, she'd come up to me and ask me gently: 'And what's with you today, Irene?'

And just that, just a little interest and affection, made me feel better. It was the nicest place I'd ever lived and the only time I felt really safe so it wasn't surprising that at the end of our allocated six weeks, I didn't want to leave.

Before the year was out, my father was back in the house, only this time he had no job so he had to sign on the dole. It caused a lot of arguments with Mammy, who was now pregnant, because she never saw any of his money. My father spent it down the bookies or the pub.

'Are you just expecting to be fed out of thin air?' my mother would goad him. 'Do you think bread, meat, potatoes – they're all free? How do you expect me to feed your enormous bloody appetite with nothing? You selfish bastard! Leaving me alone to raise your children with no sodding money. No wonder I've lost my mind!'

'Ah, quit your bloody nagging, woman!' Daddy yelled back. 'That's my money and I'll do what I want with it!'

'Why not? You've spent your whole life doing what you want. Why should now be any different? Thank God I've got Fran and Peter here to support the family or these children of yours would all be back with the nuns! You're a useless husband! Useless! I should never have bloody married you.'

'I've had enough – I'm going out.'

And then he would storm out of the house and not return until late at night. I could understand my mother getting so upset with my father. After all, he ate like a horse. It drove me mad the way he always took a massive portion of food for himself and left us children with one bowl to share between six of us.

Daddy wasn't long home before the police came for him. We had just got back from one of our visits to St Grace's when the Garda turned up at the door and ordered my father to come to the station to answer some questions. As soon as he returned Mammy poured a cup of hot tea over him.

'You stupid man!' she exploded. 'You can't do anything right!'

I heard later from Agatha that Daddy had been caught robbing the wages from the hospital at the end of our road and he was sent to prison for a year. I thought that was pretty bad – I mean, it was a hospital for *sick people*. We were told not to steal at all, but stealing from the sick? Even if he was desperate I thought that was just plain wrong. I hardly missed Daddy while he was away. Being apart for most of my childhood, I was more used to being separated from him than together.

Another year went by and we left St Grace's school for good, joining the primary school down the road. After I turned nine, Daddy was released from prison and got himself a good job as a lorry driver. Now there was another baby, Emily, in the house and the fights between my parents started up again, just like before.

I did my best to stay away from their rows and, over time, I made a few friends. One girl called Debbie lived down the street from me – her family were from England so she was an outsider in our area. We started talking one day because I was an outsider too and never had anyone to play with. She was a very pretty girl with long mousy brown hair – very tall and tough – and she was my best friend for a while, always looking out for me. She was my first real friend, sticking up for me to the other children. She didn't mind the way I was dressed or the home I came from.

Debbie came from a very loving family – she was the middle one of two brothers and three sisters and they were all very friendly and bonded. They seemed happy to be around each other and sat down every evening to tea and talked about their day. To me, it felt like this was how a family should be. They had a beautiful home – the furniture was lovely, there was wallpaper on the walls and it was always warm and clean. They introduced me to loads of new foods I'd never tasted before. At Debbie's I had my first taste of tinned spaghetti. Oh my God, it was gorgeous – really sweet and tasty, like nothing I'd ever had before. They also had tomato sauce, fish fingers and tinned pineapple. Those sharp, tangy yellow discs were like little slices of heaven. At the end of every meal at Debbie's house, I felt like I'd taken my taste buds on an exotic journey into the unknown. And I always left with a big smile on my face.

Before long, Agatha left school and started working in a sweet factory with Frances. Peter had left school at the age of twelve but he didn't have a job; more often than not he went out stealing to bring in money for our mother. She didn't mind – Peter was her blue-eyed boy. Now I was drafted in to do her jobs in the house – the washing, cooking and cleaning. When I wasn't doing the housework, I usually had my head in a magazine or a comic. I loved reading and I devoured anything and everything I could get my hands on. My teachers never thought much of me because I wasn't very well behaved in class but that didn't mean I was stupid. In fact, I loved reading and I was good at writing too. I found the work we were given in class quite easy and usually finished quickly and mucked around the rest of the time. The teacher said I didn't apply myself and lacked self-discipline but I had an idea of what I wanted to do with my life.

Over the years I'd decided that I wanted to work for a living. I wanted to make something of my life. I knew that if I got into secondary school I had the chance of learning a profession and getting a good job. But none of my siblings had been to secondary school, at least none of those that lived with us. Our eldest brother Aidan had gone to secondary school but then my granny on my father's side had brought him up and he didn't have much to do with us. I had always wondered about Aidan and why he didn't live with Mammy. One day I asked Agatha.

'He got took away from Mammy and Daddy,' she said confidentially. 'He was just a baby and Mammy and Daddy were young and didn't really know much about babies. They went out one night and they left him in their flat all alone for hours and hours until a neighbour called the police. They broke in and found Aidan there on his own crying his little eyes out. Anyways, he got took off them because they weren't looking after him right and he went to live with Granny.'

He'd been there ever since, though none of us envied him – after all, Granny could be a difficult woman and hard to please. We usually saw her once a week after Mass on Sunday and that was enough. But at least he'd never spent a day in an orphanage. And he'd got a good education, which meant that by the time I was twelve, Aidan was nineteen years old and a bus driver.

'The fact is, Irene, you won't pass so there's no point even going along,' my teacher said in her most disdainful voice when I asked her about taking the exam for secondary school. 'You're just not bright enough. Think about a factory job or staying home to help your mother. Hmmm? I think you might be more useful to your family if you were earning your keep.'

I didn't reply – I just nodded and left the classroom. The following week, and without my teacher's knowledge, I went along with Debbie to sit the exam – and two weeks later, I was sent my results. I had passed with flying colours! It gave me no end of satisfaction to take my results letter into school that day and flaunt it in front of her. She was too shocked to say anything. What could she say? I'd hoped my mother would be pleased for me but she seemed less than impressed.

'What do you want to go to secondary school for?' she

sneered. 'How's that going to help me feed and clothe you all?'

'I'll get a good job at the end of it,' I insisted. 'Then I'll have loads of money to give yous.'

'Hmmm ... fat chance,' she grumbled, and we left it there, but she didn't stop me. My granny was proud of me. None of my siblings had been to secondary school except for Aidan. Granny even bought me a new outfit to start the new school year – it was a navy smock. I loved it – it felt very grown up and smart.

'That's for getting yourself an education,' she said as she smoothed down the collar of my new dress. 'You stick with it, Irene. I've got a feeling you're a bright one.'

So aged thirteen, full of hope and excitement, I started at the secondary tech school. I had two specialist classes – tailoring and bookkeeping – as well as the usual classes in English, maths, history and religion. I loved it all – well, everything apart from religion. By now I had lost my faith in the Catholic Church. As far as I could see it was full of hypocrites and bullies, and whatever they did was just for show. Underneath, they were corrupt, nasty and evil, and all their 'holiness' and 'goodness' was just on the surface. It was an opinion I kept firmly to myself, though, since all the people I knew loved the nuns and the priests and wouldn't hear a word against them.

A very nice teacher called Mr Franklin ran my tailoring

class. He had black hair and a fussy manner but he really cared about the students, you could tell that from the start. For our first project we had to make a skirt, based around a pattern of our choice and using our own fabric. I bit my nails and fretted anxiously at the back of the class as Mr Franklin explained the different techniques we would be using to cut and sew our skirts. Then, after the bell had gone, and all the other girls had left the classroom, I approached his desk.

'I'm sorry, Mr Franklin,' I told him. 'But I can't get the material, I've got no money.'

'Don't worry, Miss Coogan,' Mr Franklin said to me respectfully. 'I have an account with one of the haberdasheries in town and if you go there and give them my name, you can order your fabric and they'll put it on my bill.'

'Are you sure, Mr Franklin?' I was overwhelmed with his kindness.

'Of course! We can't have you falling behind in class, can we?'

So I collected my black-and-white houndstooth fabric from Mr Franklin's haberdashers and used it to make a mid-calf pencil skirt. I put my heart and soul into it, and when it was done I was pleased with the result. The seams were neat, the cut was elegant and sharp, and the skirt fitted me really well. Mr Franklin seemed delighted with my work.

'That's excellent!' he said when I had finished. I blushed

at his fulsome praise – I wasn't used to it. 'You work well with the material, like you've always been doing it. Keep it up and I think you're going to do very well in this class.'

I was thrilled! I'd never been complimented in this way before. For the first time it felt like there was somebody who saw a future for me and wanted to give me a chance. That Friday afternoon, I came home from school with a spring in my step.

'Irene!' Mammy greeted me with a shout when I came in the front door. 'Will ya come in here a minute?'

'Sure, Mammy.' I walked into the living room where Mammy sat on the settee, thick plumes of cigarette smoke curling out of her nostrils.

'Irene, you're starting work on Monday,' she said, tapping the end of the cigarette on her plastic orange ashtray.

'What? What do you mean, Mammy?'

'I mean, you've got a job and it starts on Monday. So no more school.'

I couldn't believe it. My good mood evaporated in an instant – and with it, all my hopes and dreams.

'But . . . but I'm doing really well, Mammy,' I objected in a small voice. 'Mr Franklin, my tailoring teacher, he says I'm a natural. I want to stay at school, do my exams . . .'

'Yes, well, exams don't put food on our table.'

'I've just made a skirt, Mammy,' I offered limply. 'Can't I go for a little longer?'

'No! Now stop your arguing. You're going to work and there's an end to it.'

I was devastated. That weekend I hid myself away in the bedroom and cried for hours on end. There was no point arguing with my mother; I knew I could never change her mind and bringing it up again would only make her cross. Also, I knew in my heart I had a duty to my family to make sure there was enough money in the house for food and clothes. But I couldn't help it – I'd only been at school for around six months and I felt wretched about leaving. The worst part was that I didn't even have time to say goodbye to Mr Franklin or thank him for all his help and encouragement. The following Monday I started work at a paintbrush factory.

12

IRENE

⊤

Growing Up, Growing Strong

The smell from the chippy made me weak at the knees! As I stood outside, stamping my feet against the cold, I breathed in the heady aroma of deep-frying potatoes mingled with salt and vinegar. It carried down the street, and out here, right outside the shop, the scent was intoxicating.

'I'm getting meself some of those chips!' I burst out when my sisters joined me five minutes later. Fran and Aggie worked in a sweet factory up the road from the paintbrush factory, so every day we walked to work and back together. Today was Friday so each of us clutched a small wage packet. It had been a tough week, but not terrible. Each morning I was up at 6 a.m. to help out with the younger ones before leaving at 7 a.m. to walk half an hour to work, and we finished each day at 5 p.m. There was no breakfast and no money for the bus – I had to walk to work every day on an empty stomach.

The work wasn't hard – in fact, I quite enjoyed putting the glue and then the hair into the silver part of the brush head and then attaching that to the wooden handle. It was engrossing and not too difficult, and I found that the harder I worked, the less troubled I was by my thoughts. I was quicker than most of the other girls on my line so even if I finished my brush heads early, I was keen to help out the others or find more work to do. The harder I worked, the happier I was.

But holding that little brown envelope in my hand and standing outside the chippy, I could only think of one thing – buying some of those gorgeous chips!

'Oh no, you can't do that!' Agatha exclaimed.

'Mammy'll kill you if you spend your wages,' Frances echoed.

'But it's my money!' I reasoned. 'I earned it and if I want chips, I'll get chips.' I had earned myself £7 this week and a packet of chips only cost a few pennies so I couldn't see the harm. Defiantly, I marched into the chip shop and when I came out with a newspaper cone filled with chips my sisters both burst out crying. It was so daft, I couldn't help grinning at them as I dug in my wooden fork and took a mouthful. Oh, they were marvellous! Crisp on the outside, fluffy on the inside, scalding hot, salty and tangy with vinegar, I just had to have more.

'For heaven's sake,' Agatha sobbed, wiping away her tears with her threadbare gloves. 'You're going to be in so much trouble, Irene. Mammy'll beat you black and blue for this.'

'I'd like to see her try!' I smiled back. 'Now look, don't get upset. Here, have a chip!'

As we walked home, I shared the lovely chips with my sisters, though they were crying so hard I didn't think they appreciated them as much as I did. By the time we were home, we'd polished off the lot.

As we walked in, Mammy jumped up from the settee and strode towards us, her hand outstretched. Obediently, Frances handed over her wage packet – Mammy peered inside, took out ten shillings and handed that back to Frances. Ten shillings from seven punts? Was that all she got for a week's work? We were sent out to the factories with no food in our bellies, no money for bus fares, nothing, and ten shillings was our reward? My blood boiled.

Next, Agatha did the same – she handed over her wages and was given ten shillings in return. I wasn't going to stand for that. So instead of giving Mammy my wage packet, I emptied it out onto my hand and put half the money in my pocket. The rest I gave to her – three punts and ten shillings.

'What do you think you're doing?' she asked sharply.

'I'm giving you your wages,' I replied calmly.

'That's my wage packet!' she snapped.

'No,' I said patiently, though my heart was pounding. This was the first time I had stood up to my mother. 'That's *my* wage packet. You're not having it. I earned that money. You will get what I feel you're entitled to and that is all.'

Though I could feel the blood surging in my ears, I braced myself against the fear, determined not to shake, not to give myself away. I'd had enough of Mammy's bullying and her beatings. She had stopped me going to school so that I could work in the factory but I was damned if I was going to simply hand over everything I'd worked for that week. For the first time, I realized I had some power over her. If she wanted my money, if she wanted me to work for her, she had to accept it on my terms.

'I'll beat you till you're black and blue,' she growled.

'I don't care,' I shot back. 'I don't care, Mammy. I don't feel the beatings no more. I don't care what you do, you're not getting all my money.'

She stared at me for what felt like an eternity but it couldn't have lasted more than a few seconds. Then she turned away. That was it! We were all standing there, holding our breaths, waiting for her to launch herself at me but no, nothing. It was like she accepted it. And as she walked away, I breathed out with relief. I had won an important battle. I knew that, from now on, Mammy would never ask me for my wage packet again. I had wrested back a tiny bit of control and it felt good.

*

I didn't know how it happened but it seems, over the years, I had grown quite strong. Though I was still very thin and frail, I had an inner strength and I dared to look Mammy square in the eyes now and fight my corner. I discovered that instead of crying when people tried to hurt me, it made them angrier if I laughed. I had to show them they couldn't hurt me and then I had the upper hand.

I'd had enough of being weak and pitied – I was growing up and I wasn't going to be pushed around any longer. I even started to dress differently. For so long, Mammy had told me I was ugly and looked like a boy, so I decided to dress and act like a boy. I cut my hair short and I wore men's suits instead of skirts and dresses. In my dark, three-piece suits and big, clumping hobnailed boots, I felt powerful and strong. And with a little bit of money in my pocket I was more in charge of my own destiny than ever before.

But two weeks after I started work at the paintbrush factory, I was given the sack.

'I'm sorry, Irene,' the floor manager told me, scratching his head. 'I'll have to let you go.'

My heart sank – now Mammy really was going to kill me!

'Why?' I asked, confused. 'I'm a good worker, Mr Cox, the best on this floor. What have I done wrong?'

'It's nothing you've done,' he sighed. 'You're just too young. You're thirteen.'

This didn't make sense – the factory owner knew I was

thirteen when I started. In any case, it was my birthday tomorrow.

'I'll be fourteen tomorrow,' I told him.

'Yes, I know,' he said. 'I'm sacking you now but you can start back again on Monday.'

Thank God for that! It didn't seem to make sense to me but Agatha explained later that the factory owners had to pretend they didn't know when you were underage. As soon as I turned fourteen, it meant I was properly legitimate and they could put me on the payroll.

As the months passed, I started to exercise my new-found independence. Now, each weekend, I went out drinking in pubs and clubs with Agatha. Since she didn't have any money, I would buy her drinks for her. Alcohol helped numb the pain I felt inside, it made me feel invincible and let me forget about my miserable past. At home, I tried my best to protect the younger ones from the worst of Mammy's temper, and now, when Mammy took an overdose and put herself in the hospital, all us older ones rallied round to make sure the house still ran smoothly and that Cecily and Emily, our two younger sisters, stayed with us at home instead of being taken to the orphanage. Now Agatha acted like their mammy, showering them with hugs and kisses and putting them to bed at night, and I spent my wages on buying them sweets and clothes. The little ones, they were my only weakness.

To the world outside, I was somebody else, a hard girl.

I didn't let anybody get the better of me, in fact, just the opposite. If I thought somebody was going to have a go, I'd get in there first, calling them names, threatening to punch their lights out. I didn't have many friends, I didn't let people get close. Out in the world, there was nobody to help me, nobody to fight for me, so I did it all myself. And I was prepared – I sewed pockets into my suits and carried knives in them. That way, I was ready for anything.

It was worse when I'd been drinking, and most weekends I was drunk most of the time. When I'd first started drinking I was on sherry, but then I moved on to wine and lager, and then spirits like whisky and vodka. Before long, I had adapted my lifestyle to accommodate as much drinking as possible, leaving the house on Friday night and not returning until late Sunday evening. Some nights I just drank right through till the morning and, at other times, I'd go and stay at Debbie's house. We'd remained friends throughout this time, and she also worked at the factory.

Debbie stuck by me during all the nights I nearly came to blows. Most of the time I was lucky and I got away without a proper fight, though I didn't really understand why. I would be all up in someone's face, really going for it, and they would just melt away. It was rare that anyone squared up to me. I asked Debbie one night why she thought other people refused to fight me. She paused before answering, as if trying to pick her words carefully. 'It's your eyes.'

'What do you mean?'

'I mean, there's this strange look that comes over you. You look mad, proper mad, and the other person gets scared. I'll be honest with you – they think you're a bit touched. That's why they won't fight with you.'

'Well, that suits me just fine,' I replied nonchalantly, though I found her words unsettling.

Was I mad? I knew there was something strange about me, for sure. And this was brought home to me just a few weeks later when I nearly killed a girl. I was out as usual on Friday night in a club drinking and dancing with Debbie and her three brothers. At the club there was a group of sisters who came from the other side of Dublin – the Shaughnessys – I recognized their faces. The four of them were known about town as tough characters themselves, the kind of hard-faced girls you didn't mess around with. But it seemed this one Shaughnessy girl reckoned herself a bit and she had a fancy for my friend's brother Adam. But Adam wasn't interested in her – in fact, he spent most of the night chatting to me. For a while she just stood at the other end of the bar, throwing me evil looks, but then around midnight she walked up to me and whispered in my ear, 'You're nothing but a dirty slut.'

I didn't have time to think or react. A red mist came down and, a second later, I launched myself at her. I didn't know why she had called me a slut but I didn't care. All I knew at that moment was that I wanted to kill her. I felt a tug on the back of my collar – the bouncers picked us up and threw us onto the pavement outside. But I wasn't finished. Before she had a chance to move, I scrambled to my feet and threw myself on top of her, grabbing her by the shoulders and slamming her head back against the pavement. Screaming and shouting erupted all around me now, hands pulled me away, the girl's eyes rolled backwards and a dark red pool of blood grew like a crown around her hair. Sirens blared somewhere down the road.

'Get out of here!' Debbie shouted, dragging me away from the scene. 'Go on! Go!'

I took off, running up the road, and managed to grab onto the bar at the back of a double-decker bus. I sat down on the bus, shaking like a leaf.

That night I lay in bed, terrified I had killed the girl. *What has happened to me?* I'd lost control completely. All that rage inside – it was only just below the surface and it had come out in a way that I knew was dangerous. I had to avoid confrontation from now on – it was the only way to avoid killing somebody.

The next day I was a nervous wreck, fully expecting the Garda to knock on the door at any time to take me away to the cells. But nobody came. The following Monday at work, I sought out Debbie who told me the Shaughnessy girl had to have the whole of the back of her head shaved and stitched up. But no one told the police it was me who did it.

'You could have killed her,' she whispered, tears in her eyes.

'I know, I know,' I told her. 'I won't fight again. I'll make sure I find another way out.'

'You better not, Irene, or you'll end up in prison.'

So I learned another way – I learned how to talk my way out of situations, to avoid confrontation. The one person I couldn't avoid was my mother. When she was back from one of her many stays in the psychiatric hospital, she was as mean to me as ever. If she hated me before I stood up to her, she despised me now and took every opportunity to exercise her mental cruelty over me, telling me how I was an ugly person, inside and out. Ugly, mean and evil. I would breeze past her if she was in one of these moods and just mutter, 'Oh, blow it out your arse!'

'What? What did you say to me?' she'd fume, clearly working herself up for a fight. But I always pretended I didn't give two hoots about what she said.

'Nothing, Ma. I didn't say anything,' I'd sigh, going about my business. She'd be following me from room to room, jabbing at me with her finger, trying to get close enough to rile me.

'You did, you evil little cow!'

'Okay, I did then.'

And with that I'd just get the hell out of the house. I was rarely home and that seemed to suit us both. I tried not to let her see how much she affected me. I knew that it made her more mad to think that she couldn't get to me. I didn't let her know the truth, that she hurt me deeply.

By now Fran and Peter had left home and I was close to the end of my tether. I couldn't take much more but I was afraid to leave too in case she started picking on Cecily or Emily. It was like an unspoken pact between me and Agatha – the two of us created a shield around them, protecting them from our mother. If I left, Agatha couldn't do it on her own.

One day in June, shortly after I turned fifteen, I got into a fight with Mammy that pushed me to the edge. She was vile to me, as vile as she could possibly be, calling me all sorts of names and telling me how she wished I'd never been born. I felt the red mist come down and I knew in that minute I had to get away. I had to leave or I'd kill her for sure. So I ran out of the house. I ran and I ran, with just one word spinning round and round in my head: 'Freedom!' At last, I was free from her and I wasn't ever going back.

'Irene!' Martin's voice stopped me in my tracks. 'Irene! Stop! Please come back.'

I spun round – I couldn't ignore the breathless, desperate shouts of my thirteen-year-old brother.

'You've got to come back.' He had reached me now and I could sense his fear. 'Please come home, Irene. Mammy says she'll beat the living daylights out of me if you don't.'

My heart sank. Of course I couldn't let that happen.

'Please . . .'

'Alright,' I interrupted him. 'You don't have to ask again. I'll come back. Don't worry. Just . . . just go back and let her know I'll come home. I need a few minutes, okay? I just need some air.'

Martin ran back home and I stood there, staring after him. I stood there for a long time, letting my breath return to normal, trying to calm myself down. Finally, when I felt I was ready, I walked home. I came in the front door and, a second later, it slammed behind me . . . *OWWWW!*

An immense pain exploded across my back. *Jesus Christ! What the fuck was that?*

I turned round and saw my mother standing there with one of the heavy metal chains from my dad's lorry. She brought her arm up to hit me with it again so I quickly clambered to my feet and scurried away down the corridor. She came after me – her arm rose and brought the chain down again, whipping me across the back. *Owww! FUCK!!* A searing pain reverberated through my whole body.

In shock and fear, I ran, just to get away from another impact. But she ran after me, chasing me all the way down the end of the hall. I was cornered – there was nowhere to go. In a flash, something inside me snapped. I turned to face her, drew back my hand and hit her full in the face. She dropped the chain and her hand went to her cheek. She stood there, panting and holding her face. I had never hit my mother before now but this was it, there was no turning back. I pushed my face into hers, so close that I spat into her mouth.

'You will NEVER EVER raise your hand to me or these children again!' I roared. 'Do you understand? Because, I swear, if you ever hit me again I will kill you stone dead.'

For a moment, we stayed like that. My chest heaved with fury; she held her cheek, too startled to move or speak. I meant every word and she knew it. If she had made a move right then I would have killed her without a thought. After a while she turned away and retreated to the living room.

Now I had beaten her in every way – she was no longer stronger than me and, after that day, everything changed. I was the strong one now and I could do what I liked. She never hit me again and I stopped her from hitting any of the others too. Dad was next to useless. He just left my mother to get on with it, never interfering if she was picking on one of us. Though he never raised his hand to any of his girls, he didn't care what my mother did to us.

The next time she told us she was going to kill herself, I grabbed all her pill packets, threw them on the table and slammed the whisky down in front of her.

'Go on then,' I snarled. 'Do it! Do us all a favour – take the lot and do a proper job this time!'

Mammy's eyes narrowed. 'That's the devil in you again, Irene. You're pure evil, you are.'

'Yeah, yeah. Come on, old woman – get on with it and kill yourself already.'

13

IRENE

The Demon Arrives

'I don't want to leave!' Agatha yelled over the cacophony in the club. It was past one in the morning and the rock and roll band was just getting going, but I'd had enough. Agatha had dragged me along to a new club where she had arranged to meet a fella she liked. But the music was loud and dreary, the club was dull and I didn't know a soul besides Agatha. So by 1 a.m., I was ready to call it a night. Now eighteen, I had ditched the men's clothes and, just like so many girls my age in 1977, let my hair grow long. I'd even had a couple of boyfriends, but nothing serious. Tonight I was dressed in a pair of tight stonewashed jeans with a white, off-the-shoulder jumper. I gave Aggie a look of exasperation.

'Just give us another half an hour,' she pleaded. 'Then we can go.'

So I turned back to the bar and ordered another vodka and orange. Just then a tall fella with slicked black hair elbowed his way to the front of the queue and flashed me a cheeky smile.

'Hello there!' he shouted over the din. The band was well into their second set now and taking no prisoners. It was a loud, crashing kind of rock music with no discernible melody and the lead singer seemed to be wailing like he was in pain. The bloke nodded towards the stage and grinned. 'These lads are having a whale of a time. Do you think they know how bad they are?'

I smiled wryly and rubbed my arms. They ached more than usual today.

'Hey, you look like you could use a drink,' he said. 'What're you having?'

'I'm alright, thanks. I've got me own coming.'

'Great. It looks like you could use another.' He shouted at the bar lady, 'Two more of whatever she's ordered! No wait – make that three.'

Then he turned back to me. 'I'm Tom by the way.'

Somehow we managed to have a conversation over the terrible music, but I spent the whole time watching the clock, and when it got to 1.30 a.m. I told him I was leaving with my sister.

'Aw, not now!' Aggie moaned when I tapped her on the shoulder and nodded towards the door. 'Just give us another hour.'

'I'll make sure your sister gets home alright,' Tom offered to Aggie. 'You go off dancing.'

It seemed like an ideal solution – I was so desperate to escape, I agreed to let Tom walk me home. All the way back, Tom talked and talked. He told me all about himself, his family and his work on a construction site. We were talking so much, I barely noticed the direction we were heading but suddenly I realized we were walking along the canal path and there was an eerie stillness in the air around us. I was momentarily confused.

'Wait a minute.' I stopped walking. 'This isn't the way to my home . . .'

Tom clamped his hand round my mouth and pushed me to the floor. I was stunned. I tried to struggle but he was a big guy and he had his full weight on me. Out of the blue, he punched me in the face. Then again in the stomach. For a moment, I was poleaxed and just lay there in shock. Then his hand went to his ankle and the next thing he had a hunting knife and he was holding it up to my throat.

'Now don't you go screaming or nuttin,' he hissed in my ear. 'Just shut up and don't fucking move or I'll cut your bloody throat open.'

With that he pushed the tip of the knife into my neck and I felt the edge of the blade nicking my skin. I froze and then he pulled down my jeans and ripped off my knickers and forced himself inside me. Oh Jesus, the pain shot up me like a white hot poker. Every time I moved I felt the knife's point digging deeper into my neck. Laughing, he straddled me, pushing the knife up to my throat.

'You're going to die,' he rasped.

Oh no! No no no! This was sex before marriage – it was unforgivable. Now I would go to hell, now nobody would want me. I would spend my life alone and miserable.

'Just slit my throat,' I begged him. I didn't want to live any more, I didn't want to live . . .

I don't know how long I was lying there, crying in the dark, before a group of young partygoers stumbled over me on their way home. They called the police who took me to the hospital – hysterical, bloodied, beaten and with half my clothes ripped off. There, I was sedated and then taken to the police station for questioning.

At some point in the night, my father turned up. I guess the police must have called my parents but I didn't remember giving them my home details. I was shivering with shock still when they brought him in to see me. I couldn't work out what he was doing there. He didn't offer any word of comfort or affection. He just stood in the doorway, his face impassive, hopping from one foot to the other. I felt his eyes boring into me but I couldn't meet them, I felt so utterly ashamed.

'There's no point you being here,' I told him in a lifeless voice. 'Just go away.'

'I can't go,' he shrugged. 'I've got no cigarettes.'

I reached into my pocket and pulled out a half-empty

packet of cigarettes and a five-punt note: 'Here – take this and go.'

Eventually, around mid-morning, the police dropped me home and I went straight to the bathroom. There I drew a bath of scalding hot water and lay in it, scrubbing myself with the brush until my skin was red raw. Agatha tried to talk to me but I was too tired and ashamed to speak to anyone so I put myself to bed. The next day the doctor came out again and gave me another injection. The drugs were so powerful, I could barely move for the rest of the day, though in my head, I was tortured by terrifying flashbacks of the rape. *Why? Why hadn't I stopped it?* I asked myself over and over again. *Why had I let this happen to me? I should have seen it coming. I should have run away. It was all my fault.*

For the next two weeks I retreated into myself. When I closed my eyes at night, I was instantly transported back to the canal path when my attacker overwhelmed me and forced me to the ground. Then I couldn't sleep. I could feel his skin upon mine, feel his breath close to my ear and hear his heavy, sickening grunts. During the day, I couldn't face anybody, though my family were now taking it in turns to stay in the house with me. It was Martin's idea – he was devastated for me and he even tried to comfort me and put his arms round me but I couldn't accept his love. I couldn't even look at him because at sixteen – nearly seventeen – he was more like a man than a boy.

My mother knew what happened but she was no help – she never left the house much anyway. I was so deeply ashamed with what had happened and the way she acted made me feel worse. *No one will want you now,* my mind tormented me. *And no wonder – you're ugly, worthless and stupid! You've brought this all on yourself. You should have done something to stop it. You should never have let him walk you back home, you fucking eejit. You deserved it – you're an ugly, worthless piece of shit and you should never have been born.*

It felt like there was a monster in my head, a demon trying to destroy me from the inside. During all these years of heavy drinking I'd successfully managed to bury the insecurities and fears that plagued me deep down. But now there was a demon's voice inside my mind and he came at me loud and clear every minute of every day. I was helpless to prevent his destructive words from permeating my brain. I'd been so violated, I had no defences left. I couldn't sleep, I couldn't eat and I could barely stand to be in my own head any longer. There was no relief – from morning till night the voice taunted and ate away at me: *You worthless, ugly piece of shit. No one will want you. You're nothing, you're nobody. You don't deserve to live.* On and on and on it went until finally I knew there was nothing else for it.

One morning, when everyone was out of the house except for Martin, I snuck out of my bedroom and into the bathroom. There I sat down on the toilet and picked up the bottle of bleach which always sat next to the cistern. In that bottle I saw my salvation, I saw relief, a way to end the pain. That was all I wanted now, an escape from the madness that coiled itself round my brain like a boa constrictor, squeezing all the sanity from my mind. The snake in my head had wound itself tight inside my skull, refusing to let go, but somehow, somehow I had to get away. I couldn't bear to live like this any longer.

I shook the bottle – it was nearly half full, plenty for my needs – and unscrewed the cap. As I did so, I heard a pummelling on the bathroom door.

'IRENE!' Martin yelled. 'IRENE! LET ME IN FOR GOD'S SAKE!'

I tried to ignore the increasingly desperate shouts but, just as I was lifting the bottle to my lips, the door came crashing open and Martin fell in.

'STOP! IRENE! STOP RIGHT NOW!' He made a grab for the bottle and managed to knock it out of my hand and to the floor.

'NO!' I yelled in frustration and the tears sprang to my eyes. Martin had me by the wrists then and was yanking me out of the bathroom and back towards my bedroom. The next thing I knew I was back in bed and the doctor was leaning over me. He injected me again and I fell into a deep, dreamless sleep.

When they admitted me into the psychiatric hospital I weighed just five stone. For the next six months I was lost, drugged up to the eyeballs on a dizzying mixture of anti-psychotics and antidepressants. I could barely walk from one end of the corridor to the other, let alone carry on with my normal life. There was no counselling, no therapy, just a lot of drugs that left me dribbling and incapable, like a zombie. I was barely alive.

One day, the doctors sat me down and said the drugs didn't seem to be working and offered me electric shock treatment instead. The mention of it triggered a memory. I recalled that shock treatment had been given to my mother when she was unwell. It terrified me, the thought of turning into her. That night, as I lay awake, looking at the bright white moon from my bed in the ward, I resolved to get better on my own. I was not going to turn into my mother and I was not going to let my rapist win. One way or another I would get back to my senses, enough to put that bastard behind bars.

The next day, when they came to give me my meds, I only took half and I threw the other half down the toilet. That day, my mind – though still tormented – was clearer than it had been in weeks. The next day I did the same thing. A week later, my father came to take me home for the Christmas holidays. For the first time in years, I felt pleased to see him.

'Mammy never came to visit,' I observed as we rode the bus back home. 'In all the time I was in the hospital, she never came to see me.'

'Ah, you know your mother. She's busy all the time.'

I didn't buy it – if I hated my mother before, I despised her now. After all these years of demanding our pity and sympathy for her own illness she had never once shown any compassion or care about mine. My bitterness towards her was hardening into a physical lump in my chest.

As soon as I got home I threw my pills in the fire, determined to fight my way back to normality on my own. I was meant to return to hospital the next day and when I didn't the nurses came to the house with a straightjacket. As soon as I saw them at the door I bolted upstairs and hid under the bed.

'Don't let them take me!' I whimpered to my family when they came to fetch me. 'Please. I'm getting better here. I won't ever recover if you leave me in that place.'

And fortunately, for the first time in my life, my father stood up for me and agreed not to send me back. I don't know why – it was the only kind act I'd known off him. Perhaps it was because, with me not around, there was less money in the house. Perhaps he really did care. I'm not sure.

It was in the first week of January, while I was signing on at the labour exchange, that the police came to find me to tell me they had arrested my attacker and asked me to identify him in court. It was terrifying but I was determined not to let this man win. I wanted to see him behind bars. So I went to court and, as soon as I set eyes on him, my heart started to race.

'Is this the man?' the police officer asked me solemnly. I nodded.

'And can you tell us what he did to you?'

From somewhere deep inside I found the courage to look Tom straight in the eyes and say, 'You raped me and beat me black and blue and held a knife to my neck.'

In the months leading up to the trial, the police were at my door every week. They wanted to ensure I was going to go through with it. This was an open and shut case, they told me, they had enough forensic evidence from the hospital to prove I'd been raped. Of course I wasn't going to back out, I reassured them. I knew I couldn't live with myself if I let him go free and he raped another girl. Three months later, the case came to court – it took all the strength I had to give my evidence, to relive the rape in the witness box in front of all those people. It was horrible and shameful but I was determined to stay strong. All the while Tom sat in front of me, smirking. Then came the turn of the doctor – he said there was no question in his mind that I was 'forcibly entered' and his report showed I had internal bruising which could only have come from a violent rape. On the second day I was sent home by the judge who thought I might find it too upsetting to hear Tom's evidence and on day three the jury was sent out to consider their verdict.

Finally, after three nail-biting hours, we were called back in. The court was dead silent as the foreman of the jury was asked to read out the verdict, firstly, on the charge of rape.

'Not guilty.'

What? WHAT? My world collapsed. I couldn't catch my breath.

On the charge of grievous bodily harm: 'Guilty as charged.'

The grievous bodily harm charge carried a maximum penalty of seven years. The judge gave him three months, having already spent three months on remand.

The police and prosecutors were mystified. How could this have happened? How was it possible for the jury to hear all the evidence and find him not guilty of rape? I just nodded politely as they offered me their apologies – I was horrified.

They didn't believe me. The jury didn't believe me! It took me right back to the times when, as a child, I'd tried to tell my family and the doctor about the wicked things they did to us at St Grace's. They didn't believe me then and they didn't believe me now. *Why? Why didn't they believe me?* But this time I knew I wouldn't try to kill myself – no, I didn't want to go back to the mental hospital. There had to be another way.

I'd met Paul on a night at my local pub – he was tall and handsome, the sort of bloke all the girls wanted to date.

We got chatting in a big group – I knew his face but I'd never spoken to him until that night. He told me he worked cash-in-hand collecting scrap with a horse and cart, which earned him good money, and in his spare time he liked to box. He seemed steady, straightforward and kind – a nice man. From the word go, I told him all about the rape and the court case. I was terrified that because of what had happened to me, no man would want me – but Paul reassured me that he would stick by me. On our second date he told me we were going to get married. I just laughed but he said he was serious – apparently, he'd seen me before and had always wanted to ask me out. Still, I didn't take him seriously. I never thought anybody would want me. People said I was pretty but I still only saw the 'monkey face' of my childhood when I looked in the mirror.

But after the court case was over, I was desperate to make a fresh start and put all the horrors of the last year behind me. So on 15 June 1978, six weeks after the end of the court case, I married Paul. And I suppose I knew before we even exchanged our vows that something wasn't right. In my gut I knew I didn't love him.

It was so quick. Paul came from a very close family – he had four brothers and four sisters. He was in the middle out of that lot. His father was a big drinker but he was lovely, very charming; his mother didn't like me though. I think she felt we were rushing into things; it was understandable, we'd only been going out a short while and I didn't get to know her properly first.

On my wedding day, I got up as usual and cooked breakfast, then I tidied the house up. I felt very calm, very matter-of-fact. My friend Andrew, who worked at the fish market, brought up some fish that I fried for lunch with some potatoes and vegetables, just like it was a normal day. Then at around 1 p.m. Debbie arrived. By now we were both working in a sewing factory making leather coats for men. We chatted for a while and then she glanced at her watch.

'Irene, aren't you getting ready?' she asked anxiously.

'No, what's the rush? The wedding's not till two.'

'It's one-thirty now. Don't you think you ought to put your dress on?'

The truth was, I didn't want to go ahead with it. Something inside me was holding me back and I was afraid.

'Debbie,' I whispered. 'Do us a favour and get us a bottle of vodka.'

'I thought you weren't drinking today. You said . . .'

'Look, never mind what I said. Just go on and don't tell anybody.'

Later, as I stood in the church facing my groom, wearing the white dress and veil I'd borrowed from a neighbour, I couldn't help giggling. It all seemed so unlikely – me, standing here, getting married to this fellow I'd barely known for five minutes!

'Shush!' Paul hissed as the priest rebuked me with his eyes. 'This is serious!'

'I know,' I whispered, trying to compose myself. 'I know. I know. Sorry. Carry on . . .'

They thought it was a fit of nervous laughter, but the truth was, I was drunk. Not falling around drunk, just drunk enough to say my vows and get through the service. A second later, I'd forgotten what I'd said but it didn't matter, we were married and that was that. We had a small reception in the pub at the end of the street and then at 9 p.m. we left to go to my brother Peter's house for the weekend for our honeymoon. It was in a council estate in Dublin – since we had no money, it was the only place we could get away. My brother and his family had rented a caravan in Galway for the weekend.

The following day I woke up with a sore head. *Well, that's it,* I told myself. *You're married so now you don't have to live in your mother's house any longer. You're a respectable married lady and things will get better from now on.*

14

IRENE

Married Life

'Hello, you in there,' I cooed lovingly at my stomach, stroking the smooth curve of my belly. 'How are you getting along?'

It was December, just six months after our wedding, and I lay in bed, talking softly to the little baby growing inside me. I had fallen pregnant straight away and though I had always feared having children of my own, terrified that one day somebody would take them away from me, now that I was pregnant I felt wonderful. For the first time in my life, it felt like everything was going well.

At nineteen years old I was living in a small flat in Dublin city centre with my new husband, who adored me, and we were expecting our first child together, though you'd never know it from looking at me. Even six months gone I was still skinny as a rake. Just the gentle swell around my hips

186

suggested I was expecting a baby. It was a nice home with a large living room where we'd put up pink flowered wallpaper and painted the woodwork white. There was a small tiled kitchen, one bedroom and a tiny bathroom. In fact, it was the nicest place I'd ever lived.

Each morning, I laid out Paul's work clothes on the bed and made him a hearty supper every evening on his return. I no longer had to put up with my mother's vitriol, her melodramatic suicide bids or her bad temper – my home was a peaceful place, a sanctuary for us both. Paul was kind and loving to me, he gave me plenty of money for housekeeping and we were even managing to put some aside for a rainy day. I felt safe and secure.

'I can't wait to meet you,' I grinned as I patted my small bump. 'I can't wait to hold you in my arms.'

Oof! I winced as I felt an unexpected thump from inside. 'Thanks for that! Next time try kicking a bit lower down. I think you got me lungs there!'

Marriage suited me fine. I felt happy and free with Paul – I didn't know if it was love, but I was definitely content and that was good enough for now. I wasn't in any hurry and I figured my love for him would come in time.

Everything was going fine with the pregnancy until mid-January – and then I started to feel unwell. I had no energy and I felt sick all the time. I prayed that everything would be okay but then, on 22 January 1979, I went into labour two-and-a-half months early and was rushed into hospital. I didn't know what was happening – it was all too quick. My baby was born within hours but all I caught was a brief glimpse of a tiny little body, all curled up, before he was whisked away.

'A little boy!' the midwife called out, then she ran out the door with him.

'My son!' I wept. 'Where are you taking him?'

'He has to go in an incubator,' one of the nurses tried to reassure me. 'He's very small and very sick, Irene.'

I didn't get to see him properly until later that day when they wheeled me into the ward. But the moment I laid eyes on him I fell head over heels in love. I adored everything about him, from the miniature nails on his toes to the tufts of soft fluffy brown hair on his head. And yet he seemed so frail, so near to death. His little body was curled up, his skin was transparent and paper thin and he weighed just three pounds. For the first time I felt true love and I thought my heart might explode with the terrifying possibility that I could lose him before even holding him in my arms.

'They've called the priest.' Paul stared into the incubator, his face set in a grim mask. I couldn't tell what he was feeling other than fear and dread. I felt it too – a terrible gnawing dread that ate away at the pit of my stomach.

'He's called Justin,' I told my husband resolutely. 'I want his name to be Justin.'

That night the priest came to perform the last rites. I

cried the whole way through – I wanted so much to hold my baby, to cuddle him and show him how much he was loved. Lying there, with all those wires going into him, he looked so helpless and fragile. His skin was translucent, showing up every vein in his body and even the palpitations of his tiny heart.

The doctors were honest, though their words cut me to the bone. They didn't expect our son to last the night, so I kept vigil by Justin's incubator, willing him to pull through. *Please don't die, please don't die*, I called to him in my heart. Meanwhile it was all I could do to keep the demon at bay. I heard his voice now, the insidious whisper in my ear: *You don't deserve this child. You don't deserve happiness. He'll die because you're a bad person, an ugly, worthless piece of shit* . . . Inside me, the battle raged from midnight till the first light of dawn. The night nurses who came to check on Justin just saw a devoted mother, crying at her child's bedside. They didn't see the storm that raged within.

Amazingly, Justin pulled through that first night and the next night and the one after that. I sat by his bedside the whole time, watching him grow stronger and stronger, and the desire to hold him intensified with every hour. My arms ached to hold him. I talked to him every day, telling him how much I loved him and how desperate I was to take him home with me. By the third week I was convinced he was going to make it: *You're strong*, I told him. *You're a little fighter.*

You're going to come through this and you're going to be a fine, healthy young man.

Finally, I was allowed to hold him. I was shaking with excitement when the nurses tenderly placed him in my arms. But the moment his skin touched mine a peacefulness settled on my soul. I looked down at his crumpled face and breathed in his milky innocence, and then I cried. For the first time in my life they weren't tears of sadness, but of joy – I knew at that moment that I loved this child more than life itself. *I'll never let anyone take you away*, I promised my son right then and there. *I'll never let anyone hurt you.*

When they let me take Justin home, I was overjoyed. Motherhood came naturally to me. I adored Justin so much I never wanted to put him down. Though Justin wasn't an easy baby – he cried from the moment he woke up to the moment he went to sleep – I didn't mind one bit. I was sleep deprived and exhausted all the time but I could never get angry with him. If he cried, I knew it was for a reason so I picked him up and cuddled him. Paul went to work every day as usual and I spent my time with Justin. I loved having him all to myself. Occasionally I took him to my mother's but more out of duty than anything else. After the first few visits I realized she would never love my son the way I wanted her to and I got sick of watching her bored indifference towards my child.

Before long, I fell pregnant again. But I was weak and my

body had not fully recovered yet. I was still painfully thin and my hair had fallen out in places, leaving me with bald patches. Three months into the pregnancy I became ill with bronchitis and pneumonia. The doctor wanted to admit me to hospital but I couldn't bear to leave Justin so I struggled on at home and, on 15 August 1980, Philip was born. Philip went to full term but he was still only four pounds and I didn't manage to bring him home to meet his older brother until he was two weeks old. Now I was at home with the two boys to look after, still exhausted and weak, but feeling very contented and fulfilled. I had two beautiful sons and a loving husband.

Three weeks later, everything changed.

Paul had gone out with his friend at around midday one Saturday, saying he would be back for his dinner. I didn't mind – I was quite happy for him to go out and enjoy himself. But by 6 p.m. there was no sign of him. It was unusual that Paul wasn't home when he said he'd be home, but not too worrying. After all, the casserole I'd made for supper could just be heated up when he came back. But with every hour that passed, I began to get an uneasy sense of foreboding. At 10.30 p.m. I gave Philip his last feed for the night and settled him in his cot, then I sat by the window and fretted. Paul was never usually out so late. As 11.30 p.m. approached, I put a light under the casserole to warm it through. Then at midnight the door banged open and Paul stumbled inside. He was so drunk he could barely stand.

'Give me my dinner, woman!' he shouted when he saw me rising out of the armchair by the fire. He had never spoken to me like that before but I didn't argue, I just served the casserole into a bowl and put it down on the table in front of him. He stared at the dish with disgust – then picked up the bowl and threw it in the fireplace.

'What the fuck do you call that?' he yelled.

I just stood there, dumbstruck. *Who is this man?* It seemed like my husband had walked out that day and a completely different person had walked back in.

'I'm not eating that crap. I'm sick of you. What are you standing there like that for?'

And with that, his fist came flying through the air and caught me just below my left eye. Then he hit me again, on my forehead. I reeled, staggering backwards into the wooden kitchen dresser. There I stayed, too shocked to move.

Paul calmly walked out of the kitchen and into the bedroom where he immediately fell fast asleep. I remained at the dresser for a while, my chest heaving, my hand at my face, wondering what had just happened. And why? I simply couldn't understand it. Thank God our sons had been asleep! Half an hour later there came a knock on the door – Paul's friend stood in the doorway, pie-eyed, arms circling the waists of two giggling teenage girls.

'Is Paul around?' he slurred, smirking at me.

'No, he's asleep,' I answered coldly then slammed the door shut. *What the hell is going on?* I wanted to weep but I was too shocked. And then I caught sight of my face in the mirror – one eye was all swollen and black and there was a big lump on my forehead. I returned to the armchair by the fire and sat there, wondering what on earth I should do. Just twelve months earlier I might have had the strength to leave him on the spot but right at this moment, five weeks after giving birth and still weak from the pneumonia, I couldn't face it. I felt ashamed and humiliated.

The next morning Paul got up, dressed and left the house without saying a word to me. Meanwhile, Justin wasn't well; he had woken up full of cold. So I got up, I cooked, cleaned and took care of my babies. They were my priority now and nothing else mattered. When Agatha called on us, she asked what had happened and I couldn't lie.

'Right,' she announced. 'You and the kids are coming to stay with me. No arguments!'

Thank God she made the decision for me. I didn't have the strength to leave on my own. By now Agatha was twenty-six, a mum of one and living with a fella after separating from her husband. We stayed with her for a while but when I got back after a few days Paul was full of remorse, tripping over himself to apologize.

'It won't ever happen again,' he vowed. 'I love you so much, Irene. I'm so, so sorry.'

And, fool that I was, I believed him.

So I carried on as usual, washing, pressing and laying out his clothes every day, making him his dinner and taking care of the kids. On the surface it looked like everything was fine, except it wasn't. Our marriage had become a grim perversion of the fairy tale I had imagined for myself. Paul was going out every weekend now and coming back drunk just to beat me up. I learned to cover my face during these assaults – it was an instinctive thing but it didn't always work. He sometimes left visible bruises or gave me a black eye. Occasionally he apologized but often he didn't bother. Six months into this destructive pattern I found out he was seeing someone. And once again, I was too ashamed to tell anybody.

My life had taken on a new nightmarish reality. It was a cycle of drink, violence and infidelity. Agatha knew what was going on but there was nothing she could do to stop it. We saw each other once a week usually but she never mentioned the bruises – there was no point and, besides, where I lived it was normal to see a woman with bruises. That was just how some marriages were and we all thought we had to stick with it for the sake of our children. That was what the church said anyway.

Now I would dread the weekend, knowing that he

would be going out drinking and sooner or later he would be home to smash up our house and my body. Paul was a big guy and a boxer; I couldn't overpower him. If he was sober I could hold my own, but with a drink inside him his strength seemed to double.

I wanted to leave. I was desperate to take the kids and get out but the boys loved their father and I felt it was wrong to deny them the relationship. Still, I couldn't bear the thought of having any more children so I went on the Pill. I felt trapped and downtrodden. Now that Paul had a mistress to maintain, he stopped giving me money for the housekeeping. I had to get by as best I could with just our welfare payments but it wasn't easy and there were lean times when we had nothing but porridge for days on end.

Then I found out I was pregnant again. It was devastating – how could I bring another child into this terrible situation? There were times the violence got so bad I had to leave and a couple of times I took the children with me, but somehow Paul always managed to get us back home. He was sorry, he was always sorry, and he promised me over and over that it wouldn't happen again. He promised me the baby would be a fresh start for us both, he said he would turn over a new leaf. But it was lies, all lies.

Anna was born on 23 December 1982 and the two boys were delighted with their new little sister. As for me, my heart melted once more for another innocent child, and I promised to protect her for the rest of my life. But I didn't know how I planned to do this – after all, I couldn't protect myself any more from the daily beatings.

Paul went out the night before Anna's christening and when he got back he laid into me with his fists again. He got up the next day and left, missing his own daughter's christening. I stood at the altar, trying to ignore the questioning, confused looks from my family and the priest. They all wanted to know one thing – where was the child's father? But I had no answers for them. And still I took him back, scared of denying my children a father, scared of being on my own. I felt trapped – in marriage, in poverty, in motherhood. Just like my mother had been. Just like so many poor Irish women had been before me.

Not long after the christening we moved out of the flat and into our own council house in an estate outside the city centre. It was tiny and a bit like living in the Stone Ages because there was no bathroom and the toilet was outside – but I loved it. Something inside me knew that this house represented a new start in my life, a way out of my marriage. The only way to bath the children was by filling up the twin tub washing machine with water from the tap. It was a small house and very basic but I didn't care. The moment I walked in, I knew that in this house I would finally be happy. One day Paul got so drunk he put his foot through the glass of the front door. It woke the children up, who began to cry, and it was then that Justin, my eldest son, showed me that we didn't need Paul any more.

'You should leave,' he said to his father, in a voice far too mature for his years. 'We don't want you here and we don't need you here any more. I'll look after Mammy and you can go.'

From that moment I knew my children needed a stable home life more than they needed a violent father. Shortly after Justin made his Holy Communion, Paul came home one Friday after work and told me he was spending the night at his mother's house as he was off to visit his brother the next day, who was in prison for robbery. Straight away I knew he was up to his old tricks.

'If you leave now and you don't come back tonight,' I told him in a quiet, calm voice, 'then don't come back at all.'

'Yeah, yeah ... whatever!' he said as he stomped out the door. He didn't come back that night and the following morning I went into his wardrobe and got out all his clothes then shredded the lot with a pair of scissors. Every last stitch of clothing.

Then I put all his shoes in a big pile in the back garden.

'Hey, kids,' I called. 'Want to have a bonfire?'

I burned the lot.

Two days later Paul's cousin came to collect his clothes for him.

'Tell him to come himself,' I replied.

'He won't do that, Irene.'

'That's fine,' I sighed, then I went into the house and came back with two black bin bags full of the shredded clothes. There was no going back. This was it.

I borrowed a gun. I knew if he ever did come back, he was coming for my life. That first night, I sat at the upstairs window all night long with the gun. Thank God he never showed up!

As morning broke on a new day, I realized that, for the first time in years, I was free. Truly free. The following day I returned the gun.

Of course, it took a lot longer to shake off the fear that Paul would one day return to get his revenge and, for a year after that, every Friday night was spent sat at the window, waiting in readiness. If ever he was coming to get me, I knew it would be on a Friday night when he always drank the most, and I had to be prepared for him.

Over the next few months the kids and me started to relax and enjoy ourselves. Slowly, my strength and confidence returned, though it was tough at first to make ends meet. One thing I made sure of, my kids were always well fed, clean and wore decent clothes that fitted. It wasn't easy to survive on £40 a week welfare – by the time all the bills were paid I was usually skint so we had to make do with very dull food. We ate mostly porridge and stew that first year but I made every penny count and though we very rarely ate meat, there was always enough to fill our bellies.

At night I still fought the demon, but I could never give in to the depression that threatened at times to overwhelm me. After all, these kids had nobody but me and I had promised them I would never let them down. So I shrugged on my tough outer skin once more and hardened up. I was a single mother now, with all the social stigma that brought with it. I knew that people judged me, I knew that they thought there was something wrong with me, but how could I convince them I'd done nothing wrong? It felt so unfair – my husband had been a philandering, violent drunk. Why was I the one to pay with my reputation?

One thing was for sure, I wasn't going to be scared or intimidated by anyone ever again. That man had nearly destroyed me but I'd finally found the courage to throw him out. I wouldn't be bullied or beaten down ever again.

A year after Paul left for good, we were offered a bigger council house near my mother's place. Apart from the one obvious drawback of living near my mother, I didn't feel I could turn it down. Located down a quiet street, the new house had an indoor bathroom, toilet, three bedrooms and a garden, and it faced a park. I knew the children would be able to play out and have friends. This would be a fresh start for all of us, I resolved, an opportunity to make our lives even better, and two days after signing the lease we moved in. That year, aged twenty-six and a single mother of three, I enjoyed the first peaceful Christmas I had ever had.

15

IRENE AND MATT

⊤

A Connection

IRENE

'Your kids have been throwing stones at my car!' The big, muscular man stomped up the road, all pumped up and red in the face.

'MUM! MUM!' My boys Justin and Philip ran ahead of him, terrified. When they got to the front door they babbled over one another:

'He says we threw stones on his car—'

'But we never did—'

'We saw who did it—'

'It wasn't us. It was that Gemma from number twenty-three.'

'That Gemma. It was her.'

I cut them off. 'I saw it too. Don't worry – I know you didn't do it. Now get inside. Let me deal with this.'

The kids didn't wait another second, they dived into the

house behind me and I stood on my doorstep, legs splayed apart, arms folded, poised and ready for the fight. This wasn't the first time I'd had to stand up for my boys and I knew it wouldn't be the last. From the moment we had arrived on the estate my kids had been bullied, teased and used as scapegoats. We were the only single-parent family in the street and nobody liked it – they saw me as a threat. Single mothers were nothing but trouble, that's what everyone thought, and they assumed I would bring gangs, crime and violence to their homes. It was ridiculous – and horrendously unjust. I was vilified just for refusing to live with a cheat who beat me black and blue every weekend! From day one, I'd had to deal with my children coming home crying because other kids teased them for having no daddy. Now they were a target for the parents too? It wasn't right.

So I kept my eyes open – when the children played outside, I watched them. I wasn't above punishing my children if they did something wrong but I wouldn't have them getting blamed for things they didn't do. Today, I'd seen the little girl throwing the stones and I wasn't prepared to let my children become the community punchbag. The man was at my front gate now, shouting and swearing his head off. I recognized him as one of our neighbours from down the street.

'Why don't you keep your bastard kids under control?' he yelled at me, arms flying all over the place. 'Running wild! Little bastards, I'll show them the back of my hand,

I was calm when I spoke but I didn't mince my words. 'Please do not come into my garden. I'm warning you now – if you come up to my door, you won't be walking down again.'

'Where are they?' The man didn't listen to a word I said. 'I'm after giving those little runts a piece of my mind.'

'I was standing here and I saw what happened,' I told him in an even voice, though my temper was rising now. 'It wasn't my lads but that Gemma Meekin. If you want to take it up with her daddy you go ahead but you leave here now.'

'Bollocks! They need the belt to them, so they do!'

I was breathing hard now, my anger bubbling to the surface. How dare he! Who did he think he was? 'You're a big man,' I snapped, my eyes flashing. 'You're a big man and I'm just a small woman. And you think you can come here, threatening me like this? No man is ever going to raise his hand or his voice to me again!'

And with that, I picked up the axe I had hidden behind the front door and held it above my head. In that instant, I saw a vision in my mind. I could see a man in a snow-white shirt that was slowly turning red with blood. I could see it so clearly and then . . . he ran.

I stood there for a while and watched him disappear off down the road, shouting something about a 'mad woman', and for a while I couldn't move. Out of the corner of my eye I noticed a few net curtains twitching and heads shaking from side to side. I brought the axe down gently to my side. *Good! Let them see,* I thought. *They should know I'm not going to take shit from anybody.* I was a tough woman now – I kept an axe by my door and I slept with a knife under my pillow. I wasn't going to argue – that wasn't in my nature. Either they were going to walk away voluntarily or I'd kill them. He had known that – he'd seen it in my eyes.

I closed the door and went back to the kids. It was time to get their tea on. We had settled into our new life now and, though I did my best to give them a good home, underneath I was still a very angry woman. I was outraged with how the world judged me – even my own parents thought I'd brought it all on myself! There was no sympathy from them, no kindness. My father drank in the same pub as Paul and he knew, even as they bought each other rounds of pints, that Paul's own children went without.

So I put on a front, I pretended that I didn't care what anyone thought and I made sure there was always music and laughter in our house. At night and alone, I fought the demon as best I could. Ever since my admission to the mental hospital I had been on and off antidepressants, but these days they didn't work so well. The only thing that seemed to keep the misery at bay was a drink or a joint. The dope calmed me down, made me less aggressive, and even the psychiatrist I'd started to see after Paul left agreed that if it worked for me, I should just carry on. Sometimes of an evening my friend Ellie, who lived up the street, would come round and we'd drink tea, listen to music and smoke dope. That was my one way of relaxing and forgetting all my troubles.

One night, Ellie called to ask if her cousin could join us for a smoke – she confided he was on the run from the Garda and laying low at her daddy's house for a while. I didn't mind that he was a criminal – my brother Peter had been into crime for as long as I could remember. I knew it didn't make you a bad person. Peter had stolen his whole life and mainly to stop us all from starving to death. As a man he had married a woman used to the finer things in life and, to give her what she wanted, he carried out armed robberies. It was what he knew – stealing to make his loved ones happy – but of course he got caught. Most people who lived on the fringes broke the law one way or another, even if it was just buying a little hooky from the market. When you didn't have much, you had to make do.

Ellie knocked at around 8.30 p.m. that evening and behind her came a small, lithe young man with big blue eyes, long mousy brown hair and a watchful face.

'Hi, I'm Matt,' he said. His movements were graceful and smooth, like a dancer's.

'Come in,' I said. 'I'm Irene.'

We sat down for a while and had a little smoke then

Matt jumped up and started pacing. He seemed edgy and uncomfortable.

'Will you not sit down a while and have a cup of tea?' I offered.

'Ah no, I'm going off,' he replied. 'I've got to go to London.'

London? Really? I thought. *How rude! You come into my home and don't accept my hospitality? Cocky little upstart!*

'Alright, well go on then,' I replied tartly. 'There's the door – off you go.'

Matt

When I met Irene, I was twenty-two and she was twenty-nine. She was a striking-looking woman with long dark hair, a sexy laugh and a confident smile. She was outspoken but I liked that – she stood up for her kids and didn't let other people bully her. There were some folk who were scared of her but I liked Irene from the start and, when I sat and talked to her, I realized she was a good and honourable person. On our own, she dropped the attitude and she was soft and sweet. I think that's what drew us together – I saw that we were both acting these tough roles in our lives that neither of us had chosen. I'd been doing it from the day I was born, and by the time I met Irene I was sick of my life. I was sick of robbing, running and doing time. I wanted more and I knew she did too – I just didn't know how to make the change. It was Irene who saved me.

I was five years old when I first went out shoplifting. Back then, I was the second eldest son out of four kids but this changed annually until there were ten of us in total: nine boys and one girl. My mother Lilian was small and thin, with long black hair – she was easy-going and calm most of the time, except when she had a few drinks in her and then she would say exactly what she thought.

Mum kept a tidy house but it wasn't easy for her, not with my father Kieran going away all the time. As a well-known bank robber and gangster, that was just part of life for him. So when Dad was inside and there was no money coming in, I skipped school and went down the city centre to shoplift. At first I only took food – I was blatant, filling up a trolley of food in the supermarket and just walking out with it. Later on, I went into clothes shops and came out pushing whole rails of clothes which I knew I could sell for cash.

We lived in a three-storey tenement block in the middle of the city – it was a poor area but everyone knew each other and we all helped each other out. Your door was always open and there was always somebody around who would buy whatever you were selling. In my world, you did what you had to do and you never complained. That was just the way it was. Dad was always clear about that.

'You can have the criminal life or you can have the nine-to-five,' he told us kids. 'But you can't have both. And if you're going to have the criminal life then you must respect the code. You keep your mouth shut, you don't talk about stuff you do and you don't take anyone down with you.'

Dad was head of his firm – as a child I could see that he was the man in charge and I respected him for it. There were always hardened criminals in our small flat, planning their next job, as well as large bags of cash and guns lying around. When Dad was at home he provided well for the family – we had plenty of food, clothing and toys – but when he was away we just had to make do on our own. Nobody taught me how to steal, I just went out and did it. And nobody told me I had to do it – I wanted to because I knew it was my duty. As the second eldest it was my role to help my mum and to get whatever she needed. We always looked out for each other.

Getting sent down – well, that was just part of life. I got my first charge when I was eight years old, which wasn't bad considering I'd been out stealing for three years already. I was caught with a £1.90 set of Christmas lights and sent to reform school for four weeks. At the time, I felt myself swell a little with pride. It seemed very grown up to get charged, just like my daddy. I did as I was told – I kept my mouth shut and my head down. I was one of the lucky ones – as my father's son I had respect from the other boys and they left me alone, but the kids who didn't have visitors, who didn't come from known families, were bullied, beaten up and robbed every day. There were fights all the time but I tried not to get involved. I didn't enjoy Christmas much that year, away from home in a dormitory full of other boys, eating horrible food instead of my mother's home cooking.

It wasn't until I was ten years old that I began to get a sense of the limitations of my life. At first it didn't bother me that I wasn't at school but when the other kids much younger than me could read and write and I couldn't even spell my name, it was embarrassing. I stopped going to school altogether because I was too far behind to catch up. I wasn't stupid but that's how the teachers treated me and I was frustrated at times that I couldn't read letters, notices or newspapers. It was worse when I was locked up. There wasn't much to do besides read and you couldn't communicate with the outside world unless you could write, so being illiterate made me feel even more isolated and alone.

As I got older, I noticed my father fell far short of my expectations. He talked to us boys about ethics and being a good family man, but behind my mother's back he played around with other women. I knew this because I saw him in the pubs at night. I saw it with my own eyes. He even fathered a love child with another woman. This hurt because I loved my mother and she already had it hard without my dad cheating on her. But more than that, I was disappointed in my father. He was my role model, the man I'd admired and copied all my life. Yet here he was – a hypocrite and a cheat. He said one thing and did another, and I didn't like people like that. I knew early on I didn't want to grow up and be like him.

But then at twelve years old I made a terrible mistake that kept me locked in a life of crime for far too long. I got hooked on heroin. It happened so easily and so casually, almost like an accident. Today I know that becoming an addict was probably inevitable for me, considering the world I lived in. This was the early eighties – before HIV and before we even knew about the dangers of addiction. Addiction wasn't a word back then, it wasn't a *thing* the way it is today. Nowadays you can be addicted to everything from prescription pills to pornography, but in those days we didn't talk about getting addicted, we only talked about chasing the high. Heroin was cheap and readily available and most people I knew had tried it at least once. The problem was that if you did it more than a couple of times, you were hooked. It happened to me, like it happened to all my siblings and many of my friends too. We all had our own stories of how we accidentally fell into addiction.

I had been hanging around the bottom of the stairs of our tenement building when I was approached by a couple of lads I knew, both around seventeen.

'Matt! Matt!' they called me over. They looked nervous and edgy. The bigger one spoke: 'Matt, stand there and watch out for the police. We're going up the stairs here to have a turn on.'

At the time, I didn't really know what they meant by a 'turn on' but I guessed it had something to do with drugs – the way they were acting, it couldn't have been anything else. I just did what they asked me and a few minutes later the big guy came down the stairs and told me I could join them. Curious, I followed him up to the first-floor corridor where his friend sat on the floor, leaning against the stone wall, eyes closed and a serene look on his face.

'Matt, do you want some of this?' The first guy waved a syringe filled with a light brown liquid in my direction. The lads in our area always treated me like I was one of them, even though I was much younger. It was because I had been out grafting for so many years already – I don't think they even thought about my age.

'Er, no, you're alright,' I said. I really wasn't bothered about drugs. I had never even smoked a joint before, which were as common as fags in my area.

'Ah, go on,' he said, edging towards me. 'I'll give you a skin pop.'

'What's that?'

'I'll lift your skin up and just do it in there instead of your vein so it's slower. It'll sort of creep up on you.'

I shrugged – I didn't see any harm in it and I was curious to find out what it felt like so I agreed. 'Alright then, do me a skin pop.'

So he lifted up the skin on my arm and pushed in a very small amount of the liquid from his syringe. Then he made himself a tourniquet with his belt and gave himself the rest into the vein on his inner arm. One after the other, just like that. Afterwards, he let out a really long sigh and leaned back against the stone wall with his eyes closed. I just got up and walked out of the block.

For a while I didn't feel any different. But about ten minutes later, I was suddenly hit by a wave of nausea. *Oh Christ!* Saliva pooled in the bottom of my jaw, my stomach churned unpleasantly. I had to stop walking for a while to lean against a wall and then I felt a dragging sensation in my guts and I retched violently onto the pavement. The sour taste of bile filled my mouth and I spat, disgusted, into the gutter. *What is this stupid drug? Why would anyone choose to make themselves sick like this?* For a while, I stayed on that spot, leaning against the wall, breathing shakily. If I moved, I knew I was going to throw up again. I don't know how long I was stood like that before it struck me that I didn't feel so lousy any more. In fact, I felt really calm and relaxed. It was like a very nice floating feeling. And at that moment, I didn't have any cares or anxiety. *Oh, so this is why they do it!*

A few weeks later, just after I turned thirteen, I went back to the bloke who gave me the skin pop and scored a £10 bag of heroin from him. I fancied getting high again. He showed me how to cook it up and inject it into my arm and after that I took it every day. For a while it was just £10 a time but it wasn't long before it became £20, then £30 and £40 a day. Even in prison I took it daily, which meant I needed to keep robbing to fund my habit, locking me into the criminal world. By fourteen I was smoking and taking cannabis too, and was as much a hardened criminal as my father. He liked it that way – he wanted all his boys to become his little army of robbers and for a while I went along with that. I was one of his boys and, even at that young age, gangsters would approach me in pubs to ask them if I could get them guns.

At the age of sixteen I'd just got together with my first proper girlfriend when I was sent to borstal for a year. It was the hardest time I'd ever done. Normally, I was fine with being sent away because I was a 'stand-up guy'. That's what we called blokes like me who came from criminal families. I was a stand-up guy so I was okay – I got left alone. But this time I was in hell. She was free but I wasn't, and it killed me worrying about what she was up to every night. Two months in, I heard she had started seeing another bloke and it wasn't long before we split up.

After that, I tried not to get too attached – it had been torturous worrying about what my ex was up to while I was inside. So I decided it was better not to have a girlfriend at all. I didn't mind – I had heroin instead and she was a demanding mistress, sucking up all my time, money and energy.

16

IRENE AND MATT

ᴛ

Falling in Love

IRENE

I didn't see Matt again until two weeks later when he came to my door at around nine at night.

'What're you doing here?' I was surprised to see him. 'I thought you'd gone to London.'

'Ah, well, I couldn't handle it in London,' he grinned. 'Too hectic. D'ya mind if I come in?'

'Are you going to have a cup of tea this time?'

'You know I will.'

'Well, in you come then!' and I made a low mocking bow towards him, grinning. For some reason, when I bobbed up again, I caught his eyes, smiling at me, and I got a funny feeling. I couldn't work out what it was – it was almost like he had some kind of special effect on me. We smoked and talked for the next few hours – the time just seemed to fly by. I learned that Matt came from a big family and that he was not long out of prison. He was staying with his uncle now that the Garda were looking for him. For some reason, I felt comfortable in Matt's company. I knew I could talk to him and he wouldn't judge me.

Suddenly he jumped up. 'I'd better go,' he mumbled. 'I've got to be in for midnight.'

'Who are you? Bloody Cinderella?'

'No!' he laughed. 'It's me uncle. He says I've got to be in for midnight every night.'

'Well that's ridiculous!' I said. 'How old are you?'

'Twenty-two,' he replied sheepishly.

'Right! You're a grown man for God's sake. I mean, what if you want to go out dancing or, say, if you meet a girl?'

'Well I can't do that right now, not while I'm at my uncle's place. I'd love to stay, Irene, really I would, but I can't take the piss. He's doing me a big favour. Look, if you're around tomorrow night I'll come and see you then?'

'Alright, that sounds like a good idea.'

From that day on, Matt was in my house all the time. We were very happy in each other's company and the kids idolized him from the start. He was the kind of man that knelt down to speak to a child, so that they were looking at each other eye-to-eye, and really listened when they spoke. He didn't patronize and he didn't dismiss them. He respected children and they liked him for it. Of course, the neighbours all thought we were having an affair but it was nothing like that, we were just friends. I'd had a couple of boyfriends since leaving Paul but they had just annoyed me and I sent them packing early on. I suppose I didn't trust men very easily now. But it wasn't like that with Matt. I saw him as someone I could talk to and confide in – I didn't want to ruin the friendship by starting a sexual relationship.

That Christmas he turned up with a load of alcohol for me and a bag of presents for the kids.

'What did you go and do that for?' I scolded, though underneath I was deeply touched. Nobody had ever surprised me like that – or been so kind.

'I just got some bits for the kids,' he said defensively. 'It's nuttin.'

'Oh, shut up!' I said and at that moment I started to cry. I couldn't help it. I knew then that I loved Matt, that my feelings towards him were more than just friendship; I knew I wanted him in my life forever. Though he was seven years younger than me – I was twenty-nine to his twenty-two – he was more caring and mature than any other man I'd known. But still, I was afraid to tell him. I didn't want to risk our friendship. It meant too much to me.

That night he went out and he met a girl – when he told me my heart sank but I accepted it. He was a young lad after all – this girl was the same age as him and she didn't have three kids and a crazy ex-husband in tow!

'Just make sure you use protection,' I warned him. 'You don't want to get a girl into trouble.'

I reasoned that as long as I could have his friendship, then that was enough for me, so after Christmas I invited him to move into my house. I knew that people would make their own assumptions about the nature of our relationship if he moved in, but I didn't care. It was nobody else's business and it was hardly like I had any reputation to lose any more. The way I figured it – with Matt in my house, he could have his independence and come and go as he pleased while me and the kids got to spend as much time with him as possible.

He was still seeing his new girl but I didn't mind. We got closer every day. After I'd packed the kids off to school, I'd take him up a bowl of porridge and then I'd sit on his bed and we'd talk and talk. I told him all about my childhood, about my mother and being sent to the orphanage. There was a lot I couldn't talk about – stuff I had never told anyone and felt I never could. The hurt went so deep it felt too dangerous, like the stuff the nuns and staff did to me and the kids in the nursery. I didn't know how to even begin to tell him about those things – after all, when I tried to talk about it as a child, the adults all called me a liar. No, the pain of those years was buried and I was terrified of opening up to anybody. But with Matt, I was comfortable enough to give him an idea of the way my mother had treated me. He just listened quietly. For some reason, I could let my defences down with Matt, let him see the person I wanted to be, not the person I had to be.

I knew it couldn't last. In March the police came knocking.

'Open up!' they shouted through the front door. 'We've come for Matt Kelly. Come on – open up or we'll have to break the door down.'

It was upsetting for the children, seeing Matt being taken out in handcuffs. Poor Anna was beside herself. She adored Matt – she followed him everywhere, never leaving his side for a moment, even sitting outside his room until he came out. With the boys, too, he was a role model.

'You make sure you stay in school,' he told them. 'Get your education. Don't end up like me. You've got your mother here – she loves you so make her proud.'

As he was led out of the house I told him, 'You'll never go without a visitor, Matt. I'll visit every week.' He was too important in my life – I couldn't let him go.

Matt pleaded guilty to armed robbery and was sent down for seven years, which meant if he stayed out of trouble he could be out in three. I went to every court hearing and once he was sentenced, I kept to my word, visiting him in Mountjoy Prison at least once a week, sometimes more. I even did his washing and made sure he had clean shirts and trousers every week since inmates were allowed their own clothes. We always had good visits – it was hard to be inside an institution again but I knew what it was like to be locked up and I felt for Matt, losing his freedom like that, so I always made sure I was in a happy mood when I went there. We laughed and joked and the only hard bit was leaving him behind each time. Then, one day, his girlfriend came to see me with some terrible news.

The following day, I stormed into the prison. Straight away Matt could tell there was something up.

'What's wrong?' he asked.

'It's you!' I exploded. 'You're thick!'

'What?'

'What did I tell you? You don't listen to people, do you, Matt? I warned you over and over again to be very careful. Now you're going to be a daddy!'

'What?'

'You're going to be a daddy now!'

A shocked silence fell between us. Finally, Matt asked, 'How come she's not here to tell me herself? What can I do?'

'What can *you* do? You're in prison! I'll do it. I'll look after her and I'll look after the baby till you get out.'

And I did. Because I loved Matt and I wanted him to be happy, I looked after his pregnant girlfriend, buying her clothes and a pram for the baby, and supporting her as best I could. When the little girl was born, she took her to see Matt in prison. Felicity was an adorable child and she looked just like her father – I tried to help as much as possible but as the baby came up to a year old, the mother came to my door with a fella I'd never seen before.

'Matt's not Felicity's father,' she said. 'This man is.'

I couldn't help laughing in her face.

'Do you think I'm stupid?' I said. 'He couldn't possibly be the father!'

'He is – I was seeing them both.'

'Rubbish! You didn't have time.'

'I did so – anyway, you can tell Matt I won't be coming to visit him again.'

Matt took it very hard – after getting used to the idea of becoming a father he was determined to do right by his daughter. He'd confided in me that he didn't want to live the life of a criminal any more, he wanted to turn over a new leaf, for the sake of Felicity. She would be his inspiration from now on. He would change, for her.

'She's still your little girl,' I tried my best to reassure him. 'That woman is a liar and you know it. She'll always be yours and nothing she says will change that fact.'

It was over between him and the girl but he would always be Felicity's father, no matter what, and maybe one day she would want to find him. A child needs both parents. I felt strongly about that – even with my own children, I had never stopped them seeing their father. In fact, I encouraged it – the children were never in any danger from him. Whatever happens between two parents, a child deserves the love of both and I thought it was selfish to deny the child access to their parent just because of how the other felt.

*

Months went by and, as Matt recovered, I realized that now he was single there was nothing standing in my way. If I didn't say something, one day he would get out of prison and meet a new girl – then I would never be able to tell him how I really felt. And yet I was terrified that he would reject me. During one visit, I felt particularly sad about our situation. *Why can't I just tell him? Why do I insist on keeping this secret?*

'What's up with you?' he asked.

I didn't want to lie any more – I was tired of pretending. So I just blurted it out without even thinking. 'You do know I'm in love with you, don't you, Matt?'

He opened his mouth but nothing came out.

So I hurried on. 'I'm in love with you. I'm sorry but I can't help my feelings. Look, I don't expect anything from you. I don't want to lose what we have. To me, this is a life-long friendship, no matter who you are with. I'll be there for you any time you need me.'

Matt was too stunned to react – so I changed the subject and resolved not to bring it up again. I just hoped this wouldn't change things between us.

The following week I received an unexpected visitor. A man I vaguely recognized introduced himself as Leon – him and Matt had shared a cell for the last three years and he had got out two days earlier. He was here, he said, to deliver a leather jacket for Matt as he knew I brought him his clothes each week. Now that it was winter Matt would be needing a coat. But Leon also had a message: 'Irene, Matt is in love with you.'

'What are you talking about?'

'I'm telling you, Irene, the man loves you. I've spent nearly three years in prison with him. When he gets your letters or a visit from you, that's it, he's happy for the rest of the day. To be honest with you, we were all very jealous of him. There's not many with your loyalty, Irene.'

But still I didn't dare hope that he felt the same about me until our next visit, when he proved it. At first we just talked about the usual things, then I told him about his friend coming to see me but I didn't mention what he said and he didn't talk about my dramatic outpouring the week before. So I assumed that our friendship was carrying on, unchanged. But as I left to say goodbye, Matt got up – I was expecting our usual peck on the cheek but this time he took my face in his hands and kissed me fully and passionately on the lips. It was amazing and it seemed to go on forever. But eventually, I pulled away and looked at him. I was confused and wary. *Oh, don't do this to me, Matt. Don't wreck my head, don't give me false hopes!*

'I think I'm falling in love with you,' he said.

My heart soared! It was what I'd been dying to hear for so long. I walked out of that prison on cloud nine – I'd never been so happy my whole life.

*

Matt came out of prison just before Christmas and, that day, I was so nervous I didn't know what to do with myself. I'd never felt this way about anybody before. Normally I was so in control but this day I was a bundle of nerves. *What do I do? What do I say?* The next thing, he was in my kitchen. I'd never been so pleased to see someone in my whole life before and I couldn't stop grinning.

'D'ya want a cup of tea?' I asked.

'Yeah, sure,' he smiled.

My hands were shaking as I went to put the kettle on. The next thing, I felt him coming up behind me and he turned me round to face him. I was thirty-one but I felt like a teenager as he put his lips on mine and kissed me. I melted into the kiss and it was so sweet, like coming home. When we went to bed, it was intense and overpowering. This was love, true love! For the first time I had found someone who truly loved me and I loved him back. With Matt, it felt natural, as if we were made for each other.

Soon after he got out of prison, Matt moved back into my house and for a short while everything was magical.

Then I fell pregnant.

Matt

Felicity was nearly a year old when her mother told me she wasn't mine after all. Of course, I didn't believe her but she wanted to move on with another bloke and she didn't fancy the inconvenience of having her baby's father locked up.

It was devastating. If it wasn't for Irene I might have fallen apart completely. But Irene was faithful – she never stopped visiting and she wrote to me all the time. At first I struggled to read her letters, but this time I worked hard to improve my literacy. Just being able to finish a letter gave me a huge sense of accomplishment, something I hadn't felt in a long time.

Gradually, letter by letter, page by page, I fell in love. Irene's loyalty, love and devotion shone through. There wasn't a day that she didn't think about me and it meant so much to know that, even when I was away, I mattered. Nobody had ever put me first like this or had such faith in me – it was as if she could see the person I was inside, the person I wanted to be, not the person I had been up until that point.

By the time I came out of prison three years later, we were a couple and for the first time in my life I felt that I had somebody on my side who truly loved me, cared for me and wanted the best for me. What I didn't have was money and that's what I needed. So a week after I got out of prison I did a job with a couple of friends. We turned over a pub for £7,000 with a pump-action shotgun and a .38 revolver. I didn't tell Irene anything until two days later when I asked her to hold some money for me, but she didn't ask me any questions.

When she told me she was pregnant I was shocked. It was the last thing I was expecting. For a few days afterwards

I kept myself to myself, unsure how to react or what to do. In some ways I was pleased and excited, but I was frightened too. Losing Felicity had broken my heart. I couldn't bear to go through that again. But there was something different about Irene. I knew she would never betray me.

When I finally plucked up the courage to tell my family about the baby, I knew the moment the words came out of my mouth that I was really happy to be a dad again. I knew I would do it right this time. This child had a chance.

17

IRENE AND MATT

⊤

Escape

IRENE

I was devastated that I had fallen pregnant so quickly. Matt and I had only just started living together – we were still in the honeymoon phase – and, though I loved my kids madly, I honestly thought I was done with having children. My youngest, Anna, was nearly eight years old and I was relieved to have got past the early years with all of them, the intense, full-on, non-stop caring that comes with having babies and very young children. It's draining, it's difficult and it takes all your time and energy. But Matt wanted a child. I could see that. Even though he was shocked when I first told him, behind that I saw a glimmer of excitement. He had lost contact with Felicity when his girlfriend turned her back on him; he didn't want to lose this child too. I knew he yearned to be a father and I felt that I couldn't deny him.

But the news was not well received by our families. Matt's family thought he was crazy, tying himself down to an older woman and, worse, a mum-of-three. On my side, my mother insisted our relationship was just a fling. She thought that eventually I would get back together with Paul, the man who had cheated on me and beaten me up for eight years! Until Matt got out of prison, I had been round at her place a couple of times a week to help her with the cleaning and the shopping. I felt it was my duty. By now Agatha had moved out of the area, Frances lived nearby but she worked full time, while both Cecily and Emily had moved to England with their new husbands. So whenever I was round there, Mammy bent my ear about Paul, and no matter what I said she wouldn't listen when I told her there was no way we were getting back together.

After Matt got out of prison it got so bad that I stopped going round to shop and clean for her for a while. My arms had been aching a lot recently and it was the perfect excuse to stay away. Matt couldn't understand how I could be so nice to her anyway after everything she had done to me.

'Why do you keep helping her?' he asked, mystified. 'She doesn't deserve your help. She doesn't appreciate a single thing you do for her.'

It was true – my mother was curmudgeonly and un-grateful for the most part. She never thanked me for my help, she barely spoke to me half the time. I couldn't explain it – I suppose I was waiting for her to tell me that she loved me. I thought that if I did enough for her, if I helped her, she would finally come round, she would admit being horrible to me as a child and apologize. Then she would tell me that she had always loved me. That was why I went round there, that was why I kept doing things for her. But I hadn't banked on how poisonous that old witch could be. I hadn't counted on her truly nasty nature.

One Saturday, not long after we told our families about the pregnancy, Matt and I were curled up in front of the TV in the living room when there came a hammering on the front door. Philip and Anna were with their father for the weekend but Justin, who had refused to go to see his dad, was in his bedroom. I had wondered about this at the time, but I didn't force him — I thought that maybe it was a phase. Until now he'd loved spending time with his dad every weekend.

Matt and I exchanged worried looks. *Who's trying to beat the door down? Is it the police?*

There was more banging on the front door, then a voice: 'COME OUT OF THERE, YOU BASTARD!'

Paul! What was Paul doing here? The thumps at the door came harder now – there wasn't enough time.

'Move!' I quickly shoved Matt off the sofa. 'Go out the back door and over the garden fence. You've got to get out of here!'

'What? What are you talking about? I'm not going any-where.'

Matt couldn't see the problem but I had heard Paul's voice and, after years of living with this man, I sensed danger.

'He's drunk, Matt! He's not going to stop. Look, just go now and I'll sort it out, whatever it is . . .'

At that moment, Paul slammed into the door, the lock broke and my ex-husband fell into the corridor. Matt jumped up and I pushed him out the back door, then I stood in front of it, blocking Paul's way to the garden. At the same time, Paul flew into the living room, his face puce with rage.

'Where is he?' he spat. He saw me blocking the way to the garden. 'Let me through, you bitch!'

'Paul! Stop! Stop it! What the hell are you—?'

Thump! His fist made contact with my nose – the sudden impact stung and my eyes watered from the pain. Paul pushed me back onto the sofa then ran out into the garden.

'He's not there!' I yelled after him. 'Just get the hell out of my place!'

'I'll kill him!' Paul raged, nostrils flaring like a bull. 'I'll fucking kill him!'

'If you don't leave, I'll call the police.' I strode into the kitchen and held up the receiver. 'I'm warning you, Paul!'

'How can you defend him?' Paul raged.

'GET OUT!'

'How could you, you stupid bitch?!' and with that he stormed out.

Two minutes later, Justin came downstairs. I sat down shakily at the kitchen table, lit a cigarette and dabbed at my bloodied nose with my hanky.

'Mum,' he said quietly. 'Are you okay?'

For a boy of twelve, he was very sensitive and caring.

'Yes, son,' I said. 'I'm fine. Don't worry.'

Justin sat down opposite me and started to fiddle with the tablecloth.

'Mum . . . erm . . . I know why Dad came round looking for Matt.'

'Really? Well, come on then – spit it out!'

'Gran,' he said simply. 'It was Gran.'

'Oh no!' I felt a tight little knot forming in the pit of my stomach. 'No no no! What did she do? What on earth did she do?'

'Well, she asked me last week. She asked me to tell my daddy that Matt was beating up me and Philip and locking us in our rooms.'

'What? Why would she do that?'

'She told me that if I said that, Dad would get rid of Matt and you and Daddy would get back together again. But I wouldn't do it, Mum. I don't want Daddy back, and besides, Matt is very good to us and I'm not going to tell lies about him. So that's why I didn't go to see Daddy today. I didn't want to do what she told me.'

I put my arms out to my son then – he got up from the table and let me give him a cuddle. What a strong, brave boy I had raised! I was so proud of him at that minute.

'But Philip . . .' he whispered into my ear.

'I know,' I said. 'I know. Don't worry. We'll make everything right again. Don't hate your brother for this. It's not his fault.'

Later that night, when Justin was in bed, Matt snuck back in over the garden fence.

'My mother used Philip to try to get rid of you,' I told him with a heavy heart. 'She persuaded Philip that if he told his father you were beating the boys, Paul would see you off and then I would take Paul back. She tried to make Justin do it at first but he refused – that's why he wouldn't see his father this weekend. But Philip obviously took the bait.'

'What a nasty thing to do!' he exclaimed. 'Using your own children against you! It's . . . it's . . . I just don't have the words, Irene! That woman is evil. Pure evil!'

'I know . . .' I shook my head. 'I don't think I can take any more.'

Philip came home on Sunday looking miserable. I knew right away he regretted what he'd done. I had already decided I wouldn't come down hard on him – after all, he had only been a pawn in my mother's wicked games. He was a good kid but he missed his daddy – more than any of them, he longed to be with his father. Even when Paul let him down – when he failed to show up for a visit or forgot his birthday or failed to take his calls – he still wanted him more than he wanted me. Philip blamed me for 'chasing his daddy away' – how could I tell him the truth? He was ten, a child – I knew he would only hate me if I told him about his father's behaviour. But Philip wasn't allowed to tell lies. It simply wasn't acceptable and I grounded him for a week.

On Monday morning, a white envelope landed on the mat addressed to Justin. I could tell from the swirly handwriting it was from my mother. Justin opened it at the kitchen table and, as he did so, lots of little fragments of photographs fell out. I reached out to touch them and realized with horror they were all pictures of Justin that had been cut up into tiny little pieces. Pictures of him as a baby, at his christening, riding a bike, taking communion, his first school photo. They were all the pictures I had given my mother, the most precious and important moments of my son's childhood.

He passed me the letter. It was just one line long: 'I want nothing more to do with you.'

That made my mind up.

'We're not going to survive this,' I said to Matt after we'd seen the children off to school that morning. 'If we're to have any chance at this relationship, we have to leave this country. There's too much against us here. We're not free.'

'Are you kidding? This is our home!'

'But you've seen it, Matt. She's evil. She won't rest until she's destroyed us completely. Look what she's doing to my children! I won't stand by and let her do this to them or to us. Either she'll be the death of me or I'll be the death of her. One way or another, one of us will die!'

'I don't know . . .'

'Come on, Matt, we need a fresh start, we need a chance to make it work. You don't want this life either. You told me so! If we don't do this now, I don't think we'll make it.'

A few weeks later, I found myself standing on the deck of a passenger ferry, looking back at the city I had lived in my whole life. The wind whipped my skirt around my ankles as I breathed in the tangy sea air. Freedom beckoned – I could finally taste it, for real this time! Matt had gone over to Manchester the week before to find us a house while I prepared the children for the move. They were fearful and sad to leave their father and the only life they'd known, but I did my best to assuage their worries.

'After all, we won't be on our own,' I reassured them. 'Your aunties Cecily and Emily are there too.'

Cecily and Emily were both in Manchester and they helped Matt to find a private landlord while I sold off our furniture to raise a deposit.

The boat pulled out of Dublin port and I stood there, gripping the handrail, tears stinging my eyes. *Goodbye. Goodbye. Goodbye.*

'What's wrong Mammy?' Philip asked. 'Why are you crying? Are you sad?'

I looked down at my son then and smiled. 'No, son, these are happy tears,' I told him. 'I'm happy.'

He gave me a puzzled look and then ran off to join his brother and sister, on the other side of the boat, who were spitting competitively into the sea below. They were having a ball, running around the deck, exploring the different parts of the ferry. What an adventure for them! What an adventure for us all! As we crossed over the Irish Sea, I felt the tension and misery I'd carried for so long slipping off my shoulders. *Free*, I told myself. *I was finally going to be free.*

The first year in England was a struggle, but a happy one. We got ourselves secured in a rented home in the suburbs up north and settled the kids in a good local school. Matt started a course in painting and decorating while I tried to make preparations for the arrival of my fourth child, a little girl. Yes, this was a new place, an unfamiliar country, and there was so much we had to adapt to. Each night, we went to bed exhausted but happy.

At least the neighbours kept to themselves – you didn't have everyone wandering into your home all the time, poking their noses into your business. In England there was a greater sense of space and I felt like a human being for the first time, a real person. I didn't have to put on a front, I didn't have to pretend to be tough, to prove to the outside world that they couldn't hurt me. I could be the softer person I was inside. Matt, too, could be his own man, free from the expectations of the criminal world he had moved in before. In England he could live a quiet and an honest life as a devoted family man.

But the best thing about being in England was that I was finally free of my mother. I didn't have to see or speak to her and it didn't matter what she said about me because she was hundreds of miles away. In England, she had no hold over me. We kept in touch now and again – she came over when the baby was born to help out, though she was far more interested in Cecily's kids than mine. Matt was charming to her – she never saw how much he hated her underneath. As long as he only had to see her once in a blue moon, he didn't mind putting on a show. Besides, after our little girl was born, he was head-over-heels in love. Jennifer was a beautiful baby, but more than that, she represented our future. Matt was crazy about her and crazy about being a father.

So when the police came to arrest him, we were both devastated. The fact was we just hadn't moved away quick enough and a week after he had got out of prison he had been involved in a robbery. I was really upset with him about this – I'd told him when I was visiting him in prison that I wasn't planning to spend my whole life coming to see him locked up. But there was nothing I could do about it now. He was extradited back to Dublin and locked away again.

I could have fallen apart but by now I felt strong. I

packed up the family and followed him to Dublin, knowing full well that we would return to England after his release. I had no worries about my mother any more – I knew that we had an escape plan once Matt had done his time. Besides, we told everyone we were married now so they couldn't split us apart. The truth was we couldn't get married because Matt had been living under a false name but it didn't matter, we were wedded in our hearts and that meant more than any little scrap of paper.

Matt

'Manchester? Where's Manchester?' I asked alarmed when Irene first brought up the subject of moving. It might as well have been on the other side of the world! Until that moment I'd never even considered leaving Ireland for good. On the ferry on the way over I was sick with worry. I didn't know anything about this place and I'd never met Irene's sisters Cecily and Emily. Leaving all my family and everything I knew behind was hard – and yet, I felt ready for a new start. More than that, I wanted to give my unborn child a stable home life, a secure childhood and the chance of an education – all the things I had missed out on as a child. I had no idea what was waiting for me in England but I knew one thing for certain – it had to be better than what I was leaving behind . . .

There was a warrant out for my arrest by the time we left, so I went over on the ferry using a false name and we set ourselves up in a new home. I thought then about what I really wanted out of life. When I first met Irene, I was sick of my life. I had no faith in myself, my family or anyone else. All I had was heroin. I'd been in prison fourteen times already and I was on the run again, locked in a vicious circle.

Irene knew about the heroin, of course, she wasn't stupid, but she didn't know the extent of my habit. I'd always take it while I was in other people's houses or under the cover of shelter, in a derelict building or quiet doorway out of the rain. I never did it near her house. She made it clear from the start that she was against drugs but, back then, it was like an epidemic. So many friends of mine were addicts. She told me I had to come off the smack but it wasn't that simple. I couldn't see a way out. Now, four months after our arrival in England, I told Irene I was ready for the next step.

'You can do this,' Irene urged, as we lay side by side on the bed one night, holding hands. Her belly stuck straight up in the air and I kept my eye on the top of the mound for telltale signs of a kick.

'You don't need the drugs,' she went on. 'You don't need that life. You have so much more now. You can do this, I know it. I believe in you.'

It was the first time somebody had told me that I could change my life. I felt strengthened by her words and the next day we visited our GP, who referred me to a drugs counsellor. It wasn't long before I was on a methadone programme and, though it was hard at first to break the habit of smack, I was soon stable enough on the programme to come off it altogether. Best of all, it freed me from the criminal life because I no longer needed to go out robbing and stealing to fund my habit. Finally, I could relax and just be myself.

It had been hard to leave my family, and especially my dad. He didn't approve of Irene or the fact that she had three kids with another man but, worse, he didn't want me to leave Ireland and start my own life. The way he saw it, a family should stick together. There was no big argument between us, that wasn't his way. My father was subtle; he let you know what he was thinking in little ways, like his expressions and the way he acted. He said things to my brothers but he never said anything directly to me, so I only got to know what he was thinking by talking to my siblings. By the time I was twenty-three the rest of my brothers had joined his army of thieves. We were nine young healthy lads – a force to be reckoned with – and my dad knew that as long as he had his sons around him, he would always be well protected. If I left it could start an exodus – that was the way he saw it.

But I had to make my own life. I didn't belong to him and I knew, the moment I held my daughter for the first time, that I wanted to do things differently. As a father, I wanted to be there for her, for her to feel secure. I didn't want to leave her alone in the world the way my father had left me. So when I was extradited back to Ireland to serve my sentence for the pub job, it nearly killed me. I sank into a terrible depression in prison, prompting a return to smack. It was easy enough to get my hands on – usually there was a group who bribed or blackmailed an officer to get him to smuggle in the drugs. Of course, I felt eaten up by guilt for going back. All that effort to get clean had been wasted! My guilt made me want to get high even more, to escape the self-loathing that plagued me. It was a vicious circle.

Then, one day in March 1992, I found another way to escape. There was a fella four cells down from me who liked to paint. I used to wander into his cell in the daytime and watch him for hours – carefully selecting his colours, mixing them, sweeping his brush across the canvas, building up the layers and the shapes until there was an actual picture in front of him. The whole process was fascinating.

'Here, Matt, why don't you try to do a bit yourself?' he suggested during one of these extended visits.

'What? No! I wouldn't be able to do that,' I scoffed. 'I can't draw a straight line!'

Well, I had no idea if that was true or not – in fact, I had never tried painting before.

'Here.' He went over to his box of art tools and dug out some materials. 'Here's two brushes and three tubes of paint. And, okay, yes, here's a small canvas. Why don't you do something?'

I took the stuff he handed me and went back to my cell.
Why not? I might as well give it a go. So I sat down and painted
a picture from my head – it was a corner of a room with a
table and a piece of fruit on it. The next day I showed it to
my new friend.

'That's not bad for your first go.' He sounded impressed.
'Give it to us and I'll take it up to the art teacher.'

It wasn't long before word came back from the art teacher
I was to put my name down for his class right away! So
I joined the art class and started painting with the teacher,
learning different techniques from his art books and magazines. I was astonished to find that I could pretty much
copy any style that I tried. I loved the post-impressionist
style of Paul Gauguin and accurately reproduced some of
the work he did of the native women of Tahiti. I tried my
hand at some Van Gogh works and then moved on to Goya,
Renoir and even the surrealist works of Salvador Dalí.

For the first time in my life I was learning something.
I was acquiring knowledge and I was using my hands in
a creative way. It was as if my body had an innate understanding of painting, I could sense what I had to do and I
did it naturally. This was a form of escapism I had never
known before, one that actually used my brain creatively. It
was astonishing that I'd never so much as sketched before
now – it felt like I was born to paint.

The reaction I got from others when they saw my work
was amazing. I had real talent, they said appreciatively. As

the months passed, I started to develop my own style and express myself on the canvas. I gave way to my deepest, darkest emotions and created a few self-portraits with very dark, thick oils. I poured all my blackness and bitter self-loathing onto the canvas, even using my hands to paint at one point, instead of a brush. I painted the darkness inside me and the result was a very thin skull with penetrating, bloodshot eyes. Looking at that portrait, you would know there was something wrong with the artist. You could see my soul was tortured and disturbed. They were powerful images.

Irene organized an exhibition of my work, which was a huge boost, not just to my confidence, but also to my case for parole. The parole board could see I had changed and built a new life in England. 'Go back there,' they told me. 'Take your family and return to England and keep away from your old life.' So I was allowed out shortly afterwards, having served two years of a seven-year sentence. And for the first time it felt like I had a family to return to and somewhere to go.

In Ireland I was afraid to be myself for fear of people laughing at me. And showing weakness was dangerous in that world. It was the burden of being my father's son – I couldn't do anything that people would interpret as 'going soft'. But in England I'd been free to explore a different way of life. By my nature, I wasn't a tough guy and that was why

I had spent so long escaping reality through drugs. I had been living a lie. Now I could have the quiet life I wanted.

But before I returned to England, I had to do one last thing. My parents had split up – my mother finally got sick of my father's many affairs – and my mother lived on her own in the family flat; she had seen Jennifer a lot while I was in prison, which was comforting. My mum was a proud and devoted grandmother to all her grandchildren and it made me feel better to know that at least while I was locked up, my daughter was getting attention from her extended family. The one person Jennifer had never met was her granddad, my father. It was an emotional moment for me, introducing my dad to his granddaughter, but he took one look, grunted and walked out of the room without saying a word. At the time I was so angry, but a year later he died suddenly in an accident and I was comforted by the fact he had seen her at all.

Losing my father made me think a lot about what it meant to be a dad. I pored over my memories of him and tried to separate my feelings as an adult from the ones I'd had as a child. As a child I had loved and admired him without question but, the older I got, the more I saw his faults and the more I resented him for what he took from me. I loved him but I also hated him for not being there for me, for forcing me into a life of crime and for making choices in his life which hurt all of his family.

It made me think hard about the kind of father I wanted

to be. By now I was back on the methadone programme and I was determined to make it work, no matter what. Far from starting an exodus as my dad had feared, I was the only sibling in my family to leave Dublin and reject a life of crime. I didn't want my daughter following in my footsteps, the way my father had groomed me to follow him into the family business. I wanted her to have the freedom to choose her own life, I wanted her to be her own person. *Imagine what you could have been with the right opportunities*, I told myself. *Imagine the kind of life you could have had! You can give that to your child. You can right all the wrongs from the past.*

Irene

'This is the last time I ever go to prison,' he told me during one visit. 'I won't be able to leave Jennifer again. I don't care what I have to do to survive, I can't leave my little girl without a daddy.'

Jennifer was one year old when her daddy was sent to prison and, like all of us, she missed him horribly. I tried to keep us all together. Meanwhile, to help pass the time in prison, Matt took up painting and I was astonished to find he was an incredibly talented artist.

Sadly, by the time Matt was out of prison and we were preparing our return to Manchester, the boys had other ideas. Now fifteen and sixteen, they were headstrong and they had got used to being back in Ireland where they had grown up. They didn't understand my determination to leave all my family and friends, and it was hard to explain. In the end, they persuaded me to let them stay in Ireland with their father. So we crossed back on the ferry now just four of us – me and Matt, three-year-old Jennifer and Anna, who was twelve. It broke my heart to leave the boys behind but they wanted the chance to live in Ireland, the country they had grown up in. I hoped they would be happy but I couldn't stay with them. I knew I couldn't survive if I stayed behind.

Back in Manchester we picked up where we left off. I worked full time in a factory and Matt got painting and decorating jobs. Anna missed her older brothers a lot but she was happy to go back to England. She adored Matt and was so thrilled he was living at home again. Every now and again I had my dark days, but they were manageable – Jennifer gave us both hope. She was a shining light in our lives. Smart and beautiful, she astounded her nursery teachers by reading and writing at three years old. The others had done okay in school but Jennifer was bright, really bright, and I knew I wanted to give her all the chances I had been denied in my life. I wanted to give her the best education possible.

Matt and I didn't talk much about the past. Neither of us wanted to look back, only forwards. So we didn't hang photos on the walls, we didn't visit our family in Ireland and we didn't tell Jennifer about our troubled pasts. She didn't need to know – she was a child. And over here, she was free from the pressures of a society throttled by religion and poverty. We threw a protective ring around her and we prayed it would shield her from the pain and misery we had left on Ireland's shoreline.

From then on the house was much quieter, though I found it more peaceful. If Jennifer was lonely, at least she was safe. We weren't big socializers – Matt didn't drink, which was the main way of making friends in our area. A naturally private man, he seemed content to keep himself to himself. And I had one lovely friend called Pat across the street who I met at the bingo. Though Pat was twenty years older than me I felt very comfortable in her company; from the word go we were close. She was a very caring person and I saw her several times a week. Apart from Pat, we didn't make friends. It suited us that way – we had spent a lot of time in our past surrounded by others. Now it felt peaceful to be left alone.

The years passed. In the quiet of the night, the voices visited again. I had tried so hard to hide from them, to run away from them. But somehow they always found me. And after my mother died, they would not leave me alone.

18

IRENE

Reckoning

It was the call from my sister that prompted my return to Ireland.

'You better come,' said Agatha sadly. 'Things are getting bad with Mammy. She's in the hospice now and the cancer's spread everywhere.'

Matt was worried for me – he had seen how badly my mother had hurt me in the past and during our years in England, I had finally found peace, away from her.

'Are you sure about this?' he asked as I carefully folded clothes into my suitcase.

It was February 1996, Jennifer was five years old and Anna fourteen. Of course, I didn't really want to leave Matt or the kids, but I had to go for my own peace of mind. I had to give my mother one last chance to make things right.

'It's only a week,' I reasoned. 'I have to go see her now. I have to know if she's sorry. There won't be another chance to do it.'

'Well, maybe . . .' he mumbled, sounding unconvinced. 'Just don't expect too much, okay? Some people can't change.'

I spent a week in the hospice at my mother's side, returning each night to Justin's home, where he lived with his partner and her four-year-old child. I loved spending time with Justin and Katie – they were a lovely couple and very easy to be around. They were clearly devoted to each other. He was eighteen now, working on the trains – I was proud of him, he'd grown into a responsible and mature young man.

At first, I had been shocked by my mother's altered looks – she seemed shrivelled and frail in her massive bed, her hair was limp and grey, and her complexion was a sickly yellow colour. It was so different from how I remembered her – she had always taken great pride in her appearance. But there was something about the eyes that was unchanged; the beady, malevolent stare was the same as it always had been. If she was surprised to see me when I arrived, she didn't show it.

'Are you comfortable, Mammy?' I asked her each morning. 'Is there something I can get you?'

'Get me a cup of tea,' she'd rasp back. Her voice had deteriorated into a hoarse whisper. There were never any pleases or thank yous – her manners certainly hadn't improved in the years I'd been away. Though we talked about Justin, Philip, my siblings and their families, as well as her health, she never once asked me about Matt or the girls.

My father was still living in the house they had shared and I saw him very briefly, twice, when he visited my mother, but we barely exchanged five words. Looking at his dirty, dishevelled state I felt disgusted. He was like a tramp and he smelled terrible from not washing or changing his clothes.

For the most part, I just sat at her bedside and tried to help make her last days comfortable. Various family members came by at different times to drop off flowers or sit with Mammy for a while. It was nice when they were there to chat and catch up on all the family news. But when it was just the two of us, the hours dragged by. One day, Mammy got a visit from two nuns. Mammy always loved the nuns. It was strange – my experiences had been dreadful in St Grace's but still Mammy thought all nuns were saintly, wonderful people.

I had been outside having a cigarette when they'd gone into Mammy's room, and when I came back in they were sat on the chairs at her bedside. I almost recoiled in shock when I saw them. Just the sight of these ancient, wizened little women in their habits made me sick to the stomach. It was like I was being haunted by the ghosts from my past. I sat down in the corner of the room and some physical memory seemed to rise up inside my body. Without knowing it, I tried to make myself as small as possible so they wouldn't look at me or talk to me. I wanted to be invisible at that moment. I heard my mother cackling away, recalling some memory from her youth. *Leave. Please just leave!* I willed the nuns to go away. I knew it was crazy, but even as a woman of thirty-seven I felt fear at the sight of a nun.

Each day, I arrived in the hospice at 7 a.m. and left at 9 p.m. at night. Occasionally, Ma asked me to put her in the wheel-chair to take her down to the canteen for a cup of tea. She always made me take my purse, never once offering to buy me a cup herself.

'Mammy, you know I came over from England to see you,' I said one day as we sat in the canteen together. I kept my eyes on her and my voice level.

'Well you haven't been over much before now,' she retorted, looking out towards the hospice garden. She never showed any interest in what was out there, though it was a lovely place to walk around.

'But I am here now, Mammy,' I said quietly, still looking at her.

Silence.

'This tea is too weak,' she grumbled. And that was it. That was the closest we got to having an honest conversation.

Ma had medication to keep the pain at bay – I knew now that the cancer had spread to her bones and kidneys – and she spent a good few hours a day asleep. Then I would just watch her, willing her to say something to me when she woke up. It was so hard to be there with her. I wanted to ask if she was sorry for how she treated me, but it didn't feel right to prompt her. She had to *want* to apologize.

My arms still ached occasionally and now I knew why – Frances told me some years before that Mammy had broken both my arms when I was a baby. We had been talking over the phone one day about our mammy and she remarked off-hand, 'I never understood why it was always you that got the beatings.'

'Didn't she break my arm once?' It was a vague recollection backed up by regular bouts of pain over the years, which convinced me that something like this had happened.

'No, it was both arms,' she said matter-of-factly. 'She broke both your arms.'

I didn't say any more on the subject. It was too upsetting, so I just changed the conversation.

I examined the flaky skin on Ma's face and hands, the thin, weak little wrists and discoloured nails, and thought about myself as a helpless baby, lying in my pram with casts on each arm. What sort of mother breaks her own baby's arms?

Are you sorry, Mammy? Did you really mean to hurt me? I wondered. But each time her purple-tinged eyelids flickered open and she looked about her, at first confused and then finally arriving at a realization of her surroundings, she just stared right through me. No words of apology escaped those tight, dry lips, nothing except demands and instructions.

Finally, the day came when I was due to leave. It was now or never. That morning Agatha and I had gone to see Mammy together. My older sister fussed around, changing the flowers, emptying the bins, folding clothes and generally clearing up while I sat in the armchair, watching my mother. Eventually, at midday, I picked up my bag and stood by my mother's bed. She was propped up against a mountain of pillows, her eyes fixed vacantly on the TV.

'Right, I'm going home now,' I said flatly.

'Yeah, okay,' she said. *Had she heard me? Did she understand I was leaving to go back to Manchester?* Surely she must know this would be the last time we would see each other.

'I have to get the plane in two hours,' I said, my heart breaking. In the whole week I had sat by my dying mother's bedside, there had been no meaningful words between us at all. Nothing. It was as if I truly didn't matter to her.

'Okay. Bye then.'

I was calm on the outside but inside my emotions raged. I was devastated, enraged and guilty all at the same time. This was my mother, my dying mother, and I knew I should love her and should feel sad that she was dying. But I couldn't! I couldn't feel sad and I couldn't love her. I couldn't feel anything for her any more. She had demonstrated her contempt for me over and over again. I couldn't afford to throw away any more feelings on her.

Outside in the corridor, I hugged Agatha goodbye and she wished me a good journey. Then she looked back sadly towards my mother's tiny frame engulfed in the huge bed.

'It won't be long before you'll be back,' she sighed.

'What do you mean?'

'For the funeral. It won't be long now.'

I held my sister's gaze as I told her: 'I'll never go to that woman's funeral. Never! I'm not a hypocrite.'

Back at home, Matt was my rock once more as I vented all my anger and frustration.

'She had her chance, Matt! She had every opportunity and she never said a word to me,' I railed. He just listened and nodded. He had known she would never apologize.

Two weeks later, we were in the middle of packing and organizing our move to a new house when I got a call from Agatha.

'She's in a coma,' she said. 'This is it.'

There was a long pause.

'And?' I asked dispassionately.

'And . . .' Agatha stumbled, confused. 'And you're coming over, aren't you?'

'Me? No,' I said. 'No, Aggie. I have a life. I have other things to do. I'm moving into my new home soon. So no, I'm not coming to the funeral. I can't forgive her. I can't forgive her for the things she did because she never once said sorry.'

There was a long pause then.

'She didn't say sorry to you?' Agatha asked slowly.

'No. Why?'

'She said sorry to the rest of us.'

'What for?'

'For everything that happened.'

'She apologized for that?'

'Yes.'

It was like being punched in the stomach. She'd managed to say sorry to everyone else but me. Eventually, I recovered enough to speak.

'Well, that just about sums the woman up,' I laughed bitterly. 'I didn't think she had the power to hurt me any more – and look, she managed it in a bloody coma!'

She died two days later. By then we were in our new house. It was still a mess and all our belongings were in boxes but we both loved our little three-bedroom semi. It was in a quiet cul-de-sac with a big garden out the back and the high school was just a short walk away. Matt had lots of ideas for decorating and building cupboards – we'd discovered that as well as painting he was capable of doing pretty much any DIY he turned his hand to. He was still painting his own canvasses too and now he had plans to grow vegetables in our garden. When I got the call to say that she had died, I felt nothing but relief. *It's over*, I thought to myself.

That woman can't hurt me any more. Now I can let go of all the hate and bitterness and just live my life.

But it didn't work like that. The relief was momentary. I didn't feel better at all. In fact, the demons that had haunted me my entire life came to visit more often and stayed longer each time. Now, I recognized the voice straight away. It was my mother's voice.

You think you can escape? she rasped in my head. *You think you have it good now? Well, just watch what we're going to do! None of this is going to last. We're going to come and find you and destroy you. You're a horrible, nasty, evil person. You're bad luck and you know it. Matt won't stay with you. Who'd want to stay with you? What sort of person are you that you think people want to be around you? Nobody can love you. He'll leave. And when he does, I'll be here. I'll be here . . .*

The depression came back every few months and when it did I couldn't control it. My mother's voice came at me all the time, twenty-four hours a day, and after a few days, I was wrecked, wretched and ready to throw in the towel. I stopped eating and sleeping. It felt like the sharp voice stabbed at my soul, splintering it into tiny fragments, and it got harder and harder to put myself back together again. After a couple of years I stopped working, unable to hold down a job for more than a few weeks at a time before going off sick with depression. I couldn't concentrate on what I was supposed to be doing and I was starting to argue out loud with the voices, which was mortifying. There would come a point when I just couldn't leave my bed and I was constantly exhausted, all the time. Then I would have to stop working. Eventually, the work dried up for Matt too. He found it difficult to concentrate when I was in low spirits and he usually wound up at home with me, making sure I was okay. The time between each job got longer and longer until he stopped getting work altogether.

Over the years I did my best to keep the voices at bay but my life shrank when Anna left home. Now it was just me, Matt and Jennifer. I didn't go out any more. There were times I tried to write my story, but I couldn't find the words. It was only poetry that seemed to relieve the misery. For some reason I could express in poetry the pain that was locked away in my heart.

Early in 2005 my father died. Again, I felt nothing but relief when he passed on – I had tried to nurse him when his health failed in his final years and he came to live with us for six weeks, but it didn't work out. I found out he was hitting Jennifer behind my back and that was that – I told him he had to go and he went back to Ireland. I had tried to do the right thing by him – after all, he was my father – but seeing him and the way he was with Jennifer brought back so many memories. Throughout my life, he had failed to support me or take my side. He didn't deserve my love when he was alive and I certainly didn't mourn for him when he died.

At about the same time, I began to hear stories on the news and from family members about abuse scandals in Ireland. Most of them were based in Catholic orphanages or industrial schools. That same year, I saw an advert in a local newspaper. It was from a solicitor – he was looking for children who had been in various institutions in Ireland. One of them was St Grace's. The moment I saw that name in the paper my blood went cold. I had tried to put St Grace's to the back of my mind. There was too much pain associated with that place. But now my curiosity was roused and I called the number at the bottom of the advert.

'I just want to know what this is all about,' I explained to the polite young man with the Irish accent at the other end of the phone. 'It's just that I was at St Grace's as a young girl.'

'Okay,' he said. 'My name is Kane McCall and I'm one of the partners dealing with this. Can you just tell me your name please?'

After I told him, Kane asked me to hang on while he checked his files. A minute later, his voice came on the line again.

'Okay, Irene, I have your name on a list here. It seems we've been looking for you.'

My heart started to race. 'What do you mean? Why do you have my name?'

'One of the other children who was at St Grace's with you at the same time remembered you and gave us your name.'

To this day I don't know who that person was but I am grateful to them.

It was a long process but I felt that once we started I didn't want to turn back. Kane was a lovely man. I gave him a brief description of what happened to me in St Grace's over the phone that day and he insisted I visit to talk to him face to face.

When I went to meet him in the centre of town, Kane explained that he worked for a firm of Irish solicitors but was staying in Manchester for a few weeks to speak to people like myself who had been in orphanages in Ireland. Apparently there were a lot of us in the area. That first meeting took so much out of me – I hadn't talked about St Grace's since I was a child and I was ashamed and fearful at the same time. I cried and cried – but Kane was gentle and understanding.

It took a long time because I kept breaking down and I felt embarrassed because he was a man, but slowly I managed to describe all the torture I had been through as a child. I described the beatings at St Grace's, the food, the way we were made to eat our vomit, the constant humiliation like holding out the knickers on the stick, the abuse at the nursery and also the abuse at school. He was quiet for the most part, only speaking occasionally to encourage me to go on. When I stumbled or started to cry he was patient and kind, offered me tissues and told me to 'take my time'. I didn't want to give up – once I started talking I knew I had to tell him everything. All of a sudden, I could see those nuns in my head again and I wanted them punished.

'I'm sorry,' I sniffed afterwards, embarrassed about shedding so many tears. 'I'm sure you've heard worse than this.'

'Every story is bad,' he replied grimly. 'There's no one story worse than the other. If you don't want to talk, you don't have to, but please know this, Irene: I only want to help you.'

After we received all the paperwork proving that I was in St Grace's, Kane submitted my evidence to the Redress Board. A few months later a letter arrived offering me 13,000 euros compensation. Kane explained that it was a low offer because they didn't acknowledge the abuse that had taken place in the nursery or the classroom.

'I won't accept that,' I fumed. 'I don't care about the money. This isn't about the money – this is about justice and somebody taking responsibility for what happened to us in there. They didn't listen to me as a little girl. Well, they're going to listen to me now!'

And that is when I went to give evidence in person. It was unusual – Agatha, Martin and Cecily, who had been in St Grace's, had all gone through the same process and not one of them gave evidence in person. Peter, too, had been offered a settlement for the terrible abuse he'd suffered in the boy's orphanage where he'd been sent. That was why he had been so angry when he came out of the home – I didn't even know any of this until the Redress Board. None of us had talked about it. But they all accepted their offers of compensation and suggested I do the same. They told me I should put the past behind me and move on.

'I can't move on until they accept the truth,' I told Emily the night before I was due to appear before the Board. 'Otherwise all this would have been for nothing.'

When I told my three older kids about the Redress Board, they all offered to accompany me. I was grateful for their support but worried too, in case it upset them. I had never given them any details of what had happened to me in St Grace's, but thanks to the revelations in the press, they had begun to get an idea of the levels of cruelty that had been done in God's name in the orphanages. And they knew that this was important to me. As for Jennifer, she didn't have a clue what had happened to me as a young girl but I couldn't leave her out. If nothing else, it would be a nice chance for her to see her siblings. Naively, perhaps, I thought it would all be fine. I thought that with all the support I had from the professionals as well as my family, I could cope.

However, when I actually gave my evidence to the Board, they told me to my face that they didn't believe me. The Board members sat on a big long table and I sat with my barrister and solicitor at another smaller table facing them. The main Board member must have been in his sixties and he had a big bushy beard and grey hair. There was a lady and two men sat on the same table and they were all very official, wearing suits. It was very intimidating and she was the only other woman there. I sat there stunned, Kane on one side, my barrister on the other side, as the Redress Board chairman explained slowly and patiently, as if to a child, that these were nuns I was talking about.

'Nuns simply wouldn't do that,' he concluded, as if that was the end of the matter.

'Well, if that's the case, why is there a Redress Board at all then?' I fumed. 'If you are saying that I'm lying to you, why bother with all this?'

There was silence. Finally, I exploded: 'WHY? Why don't you believe me?'

The chairman cleared his throat, shuffled his papers and looked sideways at the rest of the committee members. None would look me in the eye.

'We just can't imagine that that would actually happen,' he said. 'But look, Mrs Kelly, we're happy to take further evidence if your legal team can provide it before making a final settlement offer.'

I was crying and shaking when I left. *How could they not believe me?* After all this time I had kept the truth hidden because I was afraid that nobody would believe me, just like when I was a child. I felt betrayed. Just like the jury in the rape trial, they hadn't believed me. It felt like I could never win. Nobody would ever believe me. Outside in the corridor, my solicitor and barrister were both livid.

'I'm so ashamed, Irene,' said Kane. 'On behalf of all the people in Ireland, I'm sorry for what happened to you and I'm ashamed at how you've been treated here today. It isn't right. This isn't justice.'

'It's not your fault,' I whispered, wiping the tears from my cheeks. *Why can't I stop crying?* I caught sight of my kids now, huddled in that pokey little room they'd been sitting in all day. Oh God, their faces! They looked horrified at how I was falling to pieces in front of their eyes. This was killing me! They had only known their mother to be a strong, confident woman – now they saw me weak and destroyed. The pity and fear in their faces made me despair. That night, I couldn't eat or sleep. *How could they not believe me?* I didn't understand it. I couldn't think straight, I was just desperate to get home and see Matt.

The voice crept back into my head like a virus, but I tried to keep it together for Jennifer's sake. On the flight back to Manchester, I kept myself under control. As long as I could stay strong until I got home, then it would be okay. Then I could see Matt and let it all out. It took all the will I could muster to keep my head up but the moment I got in the house and closed the front door behind me, the voice came at me, louder and stronger than ever: *They don't believe you because you're an evil, lying little bastard. You don't deserve to* be happy and you never will be. We won't allow you to be happy. We're coming for you and we're going to take you down to hell with us. There's no point fighting it any more, Irene. Just give up. GIVE UP! There's no escape.

No escape.

There was no escape.

Finally, I knew it was true.

No matter how far I ran from my past, I could never truly escape it.

There was just one option left to me now . . .

19

MATT

ᴛ

The Fall Out

MANCHESTER, 2007

What can I do? I don't know what to do. She's been downstairs crying for two days solid now and it seems nothing I say is making any difference.

I padded downstairs to the living room and stood outside the door for a few seconds, listening. The occasional sniff – I knew that meant she was still crying. I wished there was somebody I could call. I didn't know how to handle this any more. I didn't know what to do.

Irene had returned from her trip to Dublin two days ago and, from the moment she got back, she fell into my arms sobbing.

'What's up?' I asked her. I was confused – I thought she was meant to be going over there to sort everything out.

'They didn't believe me, Matt,' she gasped between sobs.

'They didn't believe me! They tried to say the stuff in the nursery didn't happen. But it did! It all happened!'

She broke down again and I hugged her tightly to me. It was all I could do.

'Shhhh,' I soothed, rubbing her back. 'Come on now, it'll pass. Let it go. Let it be done with.'

I thought after one night she would be okay, that she would get a good night's sleep and put it behind her. But on the second night, it was just the same. She was inconsolable, sobbing like a child in my arms. *Oh God, what can I do?* I couldn't take her pain away. I couldn't stop what she was thinking. Only she could do that.

'I love you,' I whispered over and over again to her. 'Things are going to be okay. Please, please. Try not to worry about it.'

'I can't stop thinking about it. It's the voices in my head,' she whispered furtively. There was a strange look in her eyes now – hunted, like a scared animal. 'They won't stop.'

'What? What are they saying?'

'I can't . . .' She shook her head. 'I don't want to talk to you.'

'Please. I want to help.'

'I can't tell you! It's all in my head.'

The next day was the same and the day after that. Each morning as Jennifer left for school, she asked me if Mum was okay and I told her the same thing every time: 'She's fine, love. She's just having a bad day.'

I didn't want her worrying about her mother – at fifteen she was still just a child. But deep down, I was at the end of my tether. Now Irene was locked away in her room and she had stopped eating again. It had never been this bad before. For the last ten years, the depressions had come on regularly every four or five months but I knew with each one that she would eventually recover and get herself back on track.

But this time – I didn't know if she was ever coming back. Now, when I looked in her eyes, I couldn't see her. It was as if the woman I knew and loved was actually disappearing. Sometimes, I'd find her huddled under a pile of coats in our bedroom or banging her head against the floor. When she wasn't crying she was talking to herself and the fear on her face never left. *I can't bear this. My beautiful, brave Irene has survived so much in her life. Now she's falling apart in front of my eyes!*

'What can I do?' I begged her one day, when I discovered her hiding in the wardrobe. When I spoke it was like she didn't even see me any more. She looked straight through me.

'Irene! Irene, please.' I put my hands on her shoulders and my fingers sank through the fabric of her clothes to sharp, angular bones. There was nothing to her any more. 'Look at me! Irene, what can I do?'

'Help me, Matt!' she whispered softly. 'Help me to stop the pain.'

'Anything!' I agreed. I was desperate. 'I'll do anything.'

'Help me die!'

'I can't do that,' I gasped, tears stinging my eyes. 'I can't do that, Irene. You know I can't.'

'If I was an animal you'd do it,' she said sadly, her eyes shining through her own tears. She smiled at me then and nodded. 'If you saw an animal suffering like this you'd put it out of its misery.'

'But you're not an animal! You're my wife and I love you!'

The next day she turned on me. 'Why?' she asked sharply as we sat in front of the TV. Her eyes flashed with anger as if I'd said something offensive.

'Why what?' I asked, but she couldn't hear me. I could see she was gone. Her eyes darted around the room, her head shook – she seemed to be listening to somebody else, but it wasn't me.

Suddenly she erupted. 'Why would you say something like that to me?'

'Please, love, I didn't say anything. It's all in your head.'

But Irene just fixed me with a steely stare and replied, 'Of course I knew you'd say that. That's what you'd like me to think, isn't it?'

I couldn't take it any more. Every time I left the house I was terrified of coming back and finding her dead. I was becoming a nervous wreck myself. What kind of life was this? Jennifer deserved better. She needed both parents and Irene needed professional help.

'Right.' I stood up. 'I'm taking you to A&E right now.

And either you come with me voluntarily or I'll call an ambulance for you. But one way or another you are going to hospital.'

Finally, she succumbed and we went to the hospital. This was way beyond my ability to cope. Jennifer was in the lounge watching TV when I told her I was taking her mother to A&E.

'She's not too well at the moment,' I explained calmly. I didn't need to alarm our daughter. 'So you just wait here while we sort this out. Don't be worrying none. She'll be fine. She just needs to see the doctor.'

She frowned and said, 'Are you sure? Do you want me to come with?'

I could see the concern in her eyes and I did my best to reassure her. 'Nah, I'm sure we won't be long. You're better off staying here. We won't be long.'

Irene was now limp and compliant as I steered her through the St Mary's corridors, towards the A&E department. When we got to the waiting room, I guided her to sit in one of the plastic chairs and approached the desk.

'My wife needs to see someone,' I said to the woman seated behind the glass.

'What's the accident?' she asked curtly. She had frizzy, busy hair and a busy manner to match.

'There's no accident.'

She looked up then from scribbling on her forms.

'No, it's not an accident,' I went on. 'She needs to see a psychiatrist. She's hearing voices.'

It wasn't long before we were shown into a small cubicle. A slight and pale doctor joined us a few minutes later. He looked like he needed a good feed and about a week's worth of sleep himself. By now Irene was crying again.

'Why are we here?' she managed between sobs. 'You . . . you . . . you know I don't like hospitals.'

But I wasn't going to be deterred.

'You see, doctor, she's going through a bad patch,' I told him. 'She's having a breakdown, hearing voices, crying all the time, won't sleep or eat. It's got really bad.'

The doctor sat down on a chair opposite us – he tried to get a look at Irene but she kept ducking away, shielding her face from him, occasionally swiping at the tears that rolled down her cheeks.

'Listen, doctor, you need to give her something to calm her down,' I went on. 'She's going to have to stay here. I can't cope with her at home any more.'

The doctor addressed himself to Irene: 'Mrs Kelly? Mrs Kelly, my name is Dr Alban. You're in hospital now, do you understand?'

Irene nodded dumbly.

'Your husband brought you here because he's worried about you. Do you think you might like to stay here for the night while we assess you?'

'NO!' Irene was vehement.

'I think it would be for the best, Mrs Kelly,' he persevered. 'We can look after you here and make sure you get some proper rest.'

But Irene was adamant, and despite the doctor's best efforts he couldn't persuade her to stay. So instead he sent us home with some Valium and organized for psychiatric nurses to come to the house to assess her.

The next morning, the nurses arrived and that's when I discovered that Irene thought her mother had taken over my body.

'I just don't understand why he would let her do that,' she told the nurse in front of me. 'He shouldn't have let her take him over like that. Now he's saying everything that she wants him to say.'

I tried to speak but no sound came out. This was unbelievable. I knew that Irene was hearing voices but I didn't know she imagined they came out of my mouth!

'We think you would benefit from some respite care,' one of the nurses suggested gently. 'This is not a hospital, Irene, it's a safe community, not far from here, where you would have your own room and your freedom. It's like a hostel. You would have therapy and access to counsellors. But best of all, you'll get some time on your own away from the house. It seems that a lot of these voices and visions that you're experiencing are wrapped up in the home environment and Matt. I think you need some time out.'

And so, that same afternoon, I accompanied Irene to the respite home where she would spend the next ten days. Luckily, it was just a short walk from our house.

'I'll call every day,' I told her. 'And if you want to see me, I'll come by with the dog. We can take a walk together.'

'Matt?' She seemed scared; her hand reached for mine.

'Don't worry,' I smiled, clasping her cold, slim fingers in mine. 'It's all going to be fine. This is for the best.'

Then I kissed her and we hugged one last time before a pleasant-looking woman in jeans and a patchwork jumper led her to her room.

'Don't worry,' the woman said as I hesitated at the door. 'We'll take good care of her here.'

And with that, I turned and walked out. As I left the building and turned onto the busy main road, I felt lighter and happier than I had done in weeks. Tears swelled behind my eyes. It was like somebody had lifted a huge weight off my shoulders and all I could feel at that moment was immense gratitude and relief. Guilt prickled at the edges of my mind – *Why do I feel so happy leaving my wife in a strange place? Shouldn't I want her at home?* No, I knew this was too much for me to deal with alone. I needed this respite as much as she did.

How have things got so bad? From the early days of knowing Irene she had told me about her difficult upbringing but I never imagined that it would lead to this. I thought that as the years passed it would get easier for her, not harder. When we first arrived in England, everything was good. We both worked, we went out at the weekends – we went to the park, to car boot sales, the cinema or out for meals. We enjoyed life. Irene had her 'dark days' occasionally but they were never that bad.

But ever since her mother died, they had got worse and worse. And now this bloody Redress Board had destroyed her mind. How could the Board ask these damaged individuals to reveal the worst experiences of their lives and then not believe them? It was cruel and inhuman.

20

MATT

᠊ᢐ᠊

The Faceless Woman

For a while I kept discus fish. Beautiful things they are, they look like their name – flat with a big, circular body – and they come in the most incredible bright colours and patterns. From the moment I first set eyes on these tropical fish in an aquarium near our home I fell in love. They were just such extraordinary creatures, like something from an alien planet. Once I got my tank and a dozen fish, I'd sit and watch them for hours, observing the way they interacted with each other, their behaviours and their group dynamics. Irene and Jennifer would catch me sitting watching these fish all the time and they'd say I was just sitting around, not doing much. But that wasn't true. Watching and observing – that's how I learn stuff.

The thing about discus fish is that they come from the Amazon and, though exquisite to look at, they are the hardest tropical fish to keep alive. They're notorious for dying from the smallest thing – which is why you have to be so careful with them. They've got to be fed a special diet in the right quantities, you've got to have the right chemicals in the water and the right sized tank. The temperature of the water has to be exactly right, the filter has to work perfectly, you've got to have the right plants in your tank and then you've got to watch them, watch them, watch them all the time for signs of illness.

Because here's the thing about discus fish – when they're ill, they don't show it. It's almost as if they hide their pain. So you can be doing everything right and thinking everything is fine and then, without knowing it, one of your fish gets sick and dies overnight. Then the dead fish infects the rest of the tank and they all go. I went through three batches of discus fish this way. I lost a dozen every time, sometimes in a few short hours. That's just how it is with these fish – the challenge is in keeping them alive. It's not like having danios, barbs, tetras or gourami or any of those standard tropical fish. Those are 'tank fillers', the non-aggressive fish that can tolerate a mixed environment, a fairly standard diet and a PH range. They're good, strong community fish, and if one or two die it doesn't usually affect the shoal. Even if it does, you can go out the next day and buy yourself a whole load more because they're not expensive and pretty much every standard aquarium stocks them. Those are the common fish that most people start with. Not me! No, I suppose it's because I'm not really interested in the easy stuff. I like a challenge.

That was always the thing about Irene – she was never an easy person but when you made her happy, it was that much more rewarding because happiness was so elusive for her. And yet there was always a deep pain that she masked from me. Like the discus fish, she hid her sickness. There is a picture that hangs in our living room called *The Faceless Woman* which I painted many years ago. It is Irene as a young woman in a black top with a white scarf at her neck. She was a beautiful woman back then – not that she ever realized it – and so alluring. The portrait is of the top half of her body and everything about it is a normal portrait except there are no features on her face. It is just a smooth blank. This was how I felt about Irene – it felt like she wore a mask all the time and her true feelings were deep below the surface. Often, I found it infuriating, as if there was a padlock to her heart and I didn't have the key to open it. The trouble was, she didn't know how to open it herself.

So all I could do was be there for her when, every four months, she would have a complete breakdown. We could be sitting watching TV and she'd be fine one minute and the next I'd turn back to find tears streaming down her face. When I asked her why, she wouldn't tell me. She refused to let me into her head. She cried, she didn't speak, she had no interest in anything, never wanted to leave the house.

On the few occasions I did go out without her, there were suicide attempts. It got to the point where I was frightened to leave her on her own, which meant the painting and decorating work dried up. That was how we ended up both out of work – Irene with her depressions and me, looking out for her.

Now I sat at home, staring at the empty tank, my last batch of discus fish having long since died. I had left Irene at the respite home a week ago and, though it was hard, I tried to keep life at home as normal as possible for Jennifer. It had only been a couple of months since they got back from Ireland and I could tell my daughter was scared at how the trip had affected her mother. I could see that, but I didn't know how to comfort her.

I have never been a big one for talking about things. Where I came from, men didn't talk about their feelings and, even though I'd changed, it still didn't come naturally to me. In any case, with Jennifer just a child, she didn't need to know the ins and outs of her mother's illness.

So, during the day, when the house was eerily quiet, I locked myself away in my studio to paint, and in the evenings I stayed downstairs, watching TV with my daughter. Occasionally the kids in Ireland rang for updates. I always tried to sound bright and positive, telling them about Irene's daily psychiatric counselling in the hospital. I didn't tell them what I learned from her GP, that she had taken so few liquids in the last few days before we went to A&E that her kidneys had stopped working properly. She was put on a special rehydration programme since she refused to have a drip. She was also given a build-up drink to help her put on weight.

Darkness crept into the room as the sun disappeared behind the rooftops and I felt the dog jump up beside me and nuzzle my hand, eager to be taken out. This was our usual time for a walk.

'Alright, girl – just give us a minute.' I stroked her head affectionately. Bess was a rescue dog, a fawn Staffie, and when we got her she was a wreck. The people who had had her before us used to beat her and so Bess was terrified of being touched. But in the year that we'd had her, she had completely changed. With love and attention, she had become the most affectionate dog I had ever known. Now, as she pawed at my leg and jumped up to lick my face, I spoke. 'I let her down, Bess. She was five stone. Her organs were failing. You know what that means? She nearly succeeded in killing herself right in front of me.'

Bess listened with her head tipped to one side – as if she really could understand me. Her eyes were full of love.

In my head, I heard myself reply: *But you got her help just in time! She needed so much more than you could ever give her. You couldn't fix her, Matt. You couldn't change what happened to her as a child.*

We had spent so long running from the past and yet it

was with us all along. I had almost let it destroy my beautiful Irene from the inside.

The last week without her had been hard. Every night I'd tossed and turned, unable to sleep without her beside me. In the mornings I opened my eyes expecting to see her next to me and my heart always sank when I remembered she was in the hostel. Now I glanced up at the clock on the wall. It was 5.45 p.m. – I had better get going. I had arranged to meet Irene for a walk at 6 p.m. that evening. So I attached the lead to Bess, who barked enthusiastically, and we walked the short distance to the hostel.

For a second, I almost didn't recognize the woman who met me at the entrance. I had braced myself to see the Irene I had left here a week before – petrified, frail and confused. But this wasn't her. This woman's cheeks were round instead of sunken in, her head was up, her hair clean and shiny, and her clothes actually clung to her body instead of hanging in sad folds. But it was her eyes! Her eyes were completely different.

'Wow! Irene!' I couldn't help smiling, and the funny thing was that this time she smiled right back. I hugged her. She was solid, not a fragile collection of bones.

I stood back to admire her and then, because I couldn't think what else to say, I said it again, 'Wow!'

'What?' she said. 'What is it?'

'It's your eyes, Irene.' I couldn't believe the difference.

'The bags have gone from under your eyes. I can see life back again.'

Irene stood there nodding.

I went on, 'You were dead, Irene. Basically you were the walking dead – there was nothing in your eyes. What a change! Your eyes are bright, your face is filling out. You look well!'

We walked together down the busy main road and then turned left onto a quiet street where there was a little park to let the dog off for a run. When we got to the entrance of the park, I leaned down to unhook the lead from Bess's collar and she bolted away. We both watched her as she bounded excitedly across the grass. I turned to look at Irene and, in that split second, I caught a sparkle in her eye and she smiled at me. My heart soared.

'I've got hope again, Matt,' she said quietly. 'This has been a good time for me. I can see now there is a way through this. I've got hope again that I can be happy and free of pain one day.'

'You nearly died, Irene.' I couldn't look at her now. 'Your body had actually started to shut down.'

'I wanted to die,' she replied, her eyes now fixed on Bess who criss-crossed the park in search of adventure. 'I was so tired that the thought of dying was the only relief I had. I'd shut my eyes and see myself as a little girl with rosy cheeks in this beautiful meadow with all these wild flowers, birds and rabbits. I was free. I was happy. There was no other human being there, it was just me. I wanted to go to that place, Matt. I wanted to be that happy little girl sitting under the tree with all the rabbits and the birds.'

It was hard for me to hear this but I knew it was true. I had seen the way she had disappeared into herself. I knew that, no matter how much I loved her, I wasn't enough to keep her alive. She had to want it too.

'The hostel, it's been so good for me,' she went on. 'I've had a complete rest and I've been able to let out all the pain. It was like my heart was broken, Matt. I've cried so much since I've been here but it's been a good crying – and the counselling has been brilliant. I know this is hard work but it's work I've got to do because, really, I don't want to die. I don't want to leave you, I don't want to leave my children or my grandchildren, and I don't want to give up fighting.'

I just listened as she spoke, the way I had always done, without interruption, without judgement.

She went on, 'A week ago I was in a lot of physical pain. It was so hard to just walk. Every bone in my body ached. At night, I didn't sleep – the pains in my stomach were horrendous and I'd stopped going to the toilet. The medication they've got me on now, it's increased my appetite. That's why I look better. I'm eating more.'

We stood there a while longer as Irene talked about the hostel and the people who were helping her – I could sense that the danger was over. She had come back from the brink.

That night I reassured Jennifer that her mum was on the mend – she seemed very relieved but, still, I didn't tell her all the ins and outs of what was happening. How could I tell our teenage daughter her mum had wanted to die?

When Irene returned three days later, she was pleased to be home but also grateful for the continuing support from her psychiatric team. She still had intensive daily counselling at the hospital and regular meetings with her psychiatrist. It was paying off – she no longer locked herself away in cupboards or banged her head against the wall, and she spent a great deal of time writing her poems and her diary. Now, when I offered her a slice of toast, she agreed to half. After a week, she was eating a whole slice and after four months she was up to a healthy nine stone. I had my Irene back again!

Then her solicitor got in touch – they had sent her psychiatric reports to the Redress Board in support of the evidence she gave at the trial and the Board had increased their offer of compensation by a few thousand euros. But there was still no admission of the nursery abuse. Irene rejected the second offer and, six months later, she returned to Dublin to appear before the Board again. I was terrified that this would jeopardize her recovery but she was determined and I couldn't do anything except support her.

'I won't be called a liar,' she said to me the night before

she left. This time Jennifer had to stay at home because she was sitting her exams, so Irene was going over on her own.

'What does the psychiatrist say?'

'She told me that I wasn't the only woman to say these things. We can't all be liars. Everything that's happened to me has happened to others too – if they call me a liar, they call us all liars. Well I won't stand for it.'

I had to admire her – the old fighting spirit was back. After all the pain and the trauma of the past six months, she wasn't going to be beaten down.

Still, on the day she was due to give her evidence again, I was a bundle of nerves. I couldn't sit still for a second and lucky Bess got three walks that day as I tried to burn off all my nervous energy. I didn't know how Irene would react if they rejected her evidence a second time – was she stronger now? Could she cope? It was so hard to say. In the past six months she had made real progress with her counselling but there were still tough days, days where she couldn't face the world, couldn't get out of bed. She was writing a lot of poetry now, which I knew helped her, but I was terrified that another rejection would tip her over the edge again.

I was on tenterhooks that evening, desperate for and yet dreading her phone call at the same time. I couldn't concentrate on anything for more than a few seconds before getting up to check and recheck the clock on the kitchen wall. Why was time dragging by so slowly?

Finally, at 8 p.m., she called.

'How did it go?' I asked straight away.

'I don't know,' Irene replied thoughtfully. If she was upset, it didn't show.

'What do you mean, you don't know?'

'Well, I said my piece. I went in there and I told my barrister that I didn't want him to speak on my behalf, I wanted to speak for myself. And I did – even though I was nervous, you know, really nervous. I told them, "Look, you can call me a liar all you want but I know the facts. I know what's happened to me. I was there. And I haven't come here looking for money. You can shove your money. I want an apology, a public apology."'

'What did they say?'

'They said, "Oh, so you're expecting us to go public and say we're very sorry, Irene?" I said, "No, I want those nuns to take responsibility for what they did to us because they're getting away with murder. Not one nun has been arrested, not one nun has come forward," and "yes, these things did happen." They're still denying it!'

'Oh wow! Irene, you really gave it to them!' I was so impressed. It must have been so hard for her to get up and say those things to the Board.

'I did, Matt. I did. So then they said. "Well, we're sorry." But they didn't sound sorry. They said it very matter-of-factly. And then they said they believed me because they had seen more women who had said the same thing.'

'They believe you, Irene. That's brilliant!' It was a huge relief to hear that. I couldn't imagine the people on that Board had any idea how much Irene's sanity and our home life relied on that.

'Yes, the barrister says we'll get another offer now. But it's not about the money – I just want somebody to take responsibility for what happened.'

'Well, maybe they will now.'

'I hope so.'

Irene was home the next day and I was waiting with a cup of tea and a big hug – I was so proud of her! Just a week later she accepted an offer of 22,000 euros compensation which she couldn't give away quick enough. She gave it to the kids and treated the grandkids.

I overheard her on the phone to Anna one night, who felt bad about taking her mother's money.

'Don't be silly,' Irene was saying. 'I WANT to give it to you.'

Silence as she listened. I knew all the kids felt the same about this; their mother had gone through hell for this compensation. What right did they have to take it off her? But as I explained to them myself, it was never about the money for Irene. She could never have spent it on herself anyway, even if she wanted to. Irene didn't want anything to do with the money. As far as she was concerned, the money was tainted – it represented a childhood destroyed by evil.

Now she was quite cross.

'Look, Anna,' I heard her from the kitchen. 'If it's my money to do what I want with then what I want to do is spend it on my children and my grandchildren. I don't get that sort of opportunity every day so really you've got no right to tell me I can't.'

It was only after she had spent it that we found out it was hush money, meant to buy her silence. Until the Redress Board published their report in 2009, we didn't know that by accepting the money she could never speak publicly about what happened to her. That she could never identify the people who did it or even the place where it happened. When they signed all the papers for the compensation, she was aware of the fact that she was signing away her right to a private prosecution but she had no idea the contract included a confidentiality clause which prevented her going public. She thought that when the report came out all the evidence would come out too and the nuns would be punished. She was wrong.

Under the terms of the compensation package, no nun, priest or member of staff in the orphanages could be publicly named or identified. The Catholic orders had done a deal with the government, which meant they couldn't be prosecuted. So when the Ryan Report came out detailing all the abuses in 250 institutions and involving thousands of children, it didn't name the abusers either. The nuns and the priests that had terrorized children for decades – beating them, raping them, torturing and humiliating them – they all got away with it.

Irene, like so many who gave evidence, felt betrayed. If I had lost faith with the Catholic Church before then, I hated them afterwards. They had failed to live up to their own teachings and then, when they had been found out, they'd tried to cover it up. It was disgusting and hypocritical. What right did they have to tell anybody else what to do any more? They were finished. Morally bankrupt.

But that wasn't the end of the story. The fact was that, by their actions, these nuns and priests had created a generation of very damaged individuals. When these people got their compensation and they realized they weren't going to get real justice, they killed themselves. We watched it happen in front of our eyes. There were men and women we knew, like Irene, who had gone through the rigors of the Redress system, bringing up all that pain again, only to be told that nobody would get punished. It was too much and they overdosed on drugs or drank themselves to death. The tragedy played out over and over again.

It was far from the end of the story for us, either. Irene

was still battling her demons and, unknown to us, our own daughter was suffering too.

When she was a little girl Jennifer was by my side the whole time; we were inseparable. She followed me about like my shadow, helping me with all the little jobs around the house, never leaving my side. I was so charmed by her and thrilled to be able to teach her and help her develop her talents. It wasn't a selfless act – it fed my own soul to nurture her.

There was an unspoken agreement between Irene and myself – we were leaving the past behind so our daughter didn't need to know about our old lives and, in time, she learned not to ask. As Jennifer got older and excelled in school I became stricter, keen to push her as far as she could go and help her avoid the troubles that childhood can bring. I returned to Ireland occasionally for family funerals but I never stayed long and I never took Jennifer. She was innocent and I wanted her to stay that way as long as possible. Occasionally she went to stay with her Aunt Emily on Irene's side, but I didn't want her mixing with my family too much.

Neither Irene nor I had had a proper childhood so we were determined to give that to Jennifer. We thought she was happy, we thought she had everything she could possibly want. But as time went on and she began to push at the boundaries, it became harder and harder to explain that we were only trying to do our best for her. I wanted to give her freedom as an adult – freedom to choose her own place in the world. But she definitely didn't see it that way.

We had worked so hard to protect Jennifer from our pain but in the end we became like strangers to each other. In 2010, just after starting her medical science degree at Manchester University, she moved into her own flat. I was so proud of her and proud of everything she had achieved. I thought we had done it – we had managed to break the cycle of our past. She had achieved freedom. Only it came at a cost . . .

21

JENNIFER

⊤

Understanding

MANCHESTER, 2010

'Will you meet me in town?' It was rare for Mum to call me up, but even more unusual for her to ask to meet me anywhere. I had been living on my own for the past five months and it irked me that her and Dad had only visited once.

Now nineteen, I lived in a small, one-bedroom flat with my boyfriend Arnie, just on the outskirts of town. It had been exciting moving out but the day itself was tinged with sadness. Dad had refused to come and help me with the move so in the end I had made three journeys in Arnie's car to get all my stuff and I hung all my own pictures. Now I was constantly on the go, trying to keep up with my studies, and waitressing nights and on the weekend to pay the rent and the bills. Most nights I fell into bed completely exhausted. There were no wild freshers' parties for me, no drunken nights on the town – I didn't really drink and, in any case, I needed to save every penny to pay the bills.

'You're so boring!' complained my friend Kim one day after I turned down an invitation to her house party. 'You never want to do anything!'

'I can't help it!' I shot back defensively. 'I've got to work. I don't really have any choice in the matter.'

I was rattled by her accusation, but also resentful. I couldn't afford to be exciting. I didn't have wealthy parents supporting my years through college like Kim. Her parents gave her enough money to live off in the term time and then she went home in the holidays where she picked up her easy part-time job to buy herself nice clothes. In Kim's world, going to university was normal, expected even. But to my family it was amazing – nobody in my family had ever been to university, most of them hadn't even finished school. I knew my parents had been very proud of me when I'd got into Manchester University to study medical science, they just didn't have the money to help me out. Both on benefits, they struggled to make ends meet.

I was desperate to leave home as soon as I turned eighteen. I wanted to live my own life, away from my parents and their strict rules. I had bought myself driving lessons and passed my test first time, and now that I was with Arnie it felt like we needed our own space. Dad had spent so long forbidding me to have relationships that he couldn't get his head around the idea of my boyfriend coming to spend the evening with us. Just sitting in front of the TV with them both was unbearably awkward and I knew Dad didn't trust Arnie. He made his feelings perfectly clear, even if he never spoke. So I think it was a relief to everyone when I told my parents I was moving out.

They couldn't say anything – I'd done everything they'd asked of me. I had stayed in school, out of trouble and worked hard, achieving two As and two Bs in my A levels. When I got my results through, I was ecstatic. I showed Dad and he gave me a half-hearted pat on the shoulder. I couldn't remember the last time I had hugged either one of them. Arnie said I wasn't a cuddly sort of person and it made me realize that he was right. Growing up without physical affection from my parents had made me that way, and even though my sister had liked to hug me, she'd left home years before, so I got used to keeping my distance. I shied away from touching people and loathed public displays of emotion.

Now I sat at a window seat in McDonald's, sipping at my tap water and watching the busy street thrumming with activity. It had taken two buses to get into town and it annoyed me a little that she hadn't wanted to come to the flat. After all these years controlling my every move, it was like I had moved out and they had forgotten all about me! I glanced impatiently at my watch – another three hours before I had to start work in the hotel restaurant near my home. I was on late shift so that meant I wouldn't get in before midnight tonight. I sighed – I'd already done a full day of classes and now I was looking at doing another full day's worth of work.

Mum was ten minutes late and, when she found me by the window, she seemed edgy and nervous.

'I have to go to a therapy session with a nurse,' she explained. 'They need to assess me for my disability allowance. It's not far from here – would you like to come?'

'Okay,' I shrugged. I hadn't planned on spending my only spare hours this week in a therapy session but then, this whole meeting was odd and out of character. Mum never invited me to go anywhere, let alone her therapy. She still didn't like to talk about her past, despite having a full-on breakdown after we got back from Ireland in 2007. She didn't even like to mention the fact that she'd had a breakdown at all, though of course I knew she had got money from the Redress Board for the things that she suffered in the orphanage. I didn't know anything more than that, though. I just guessed it must have been serious because they gave her a lot of money and no organization gives away thousands of pounds for nothing.

At the time, Dad had played it down, telling me Mum was going away for a rest and she'd be back when she was feeling a bit better. He made out that this was all very normal and I wasn't to worry because he wasn't worried. He drove me mad sometimes – I had *seen* her! She was a complete wreck!

And of course I worried about her. I didn't want to lose my mum – I knew that people who were depressed did stupid things like try to top themselves. I also knew that Mum was worryingly thin. But no one talked to me about her illness and their refusal to include me made me feel like an unwelcome intruder in their lives. In the end I didn't bother asking for information, I just counted the days until I could leave home and start my life on my own.

Mum and I chatted on the way to the clinic for her appointment – she asked if my coat was new and I told her pointedly that I hadn't bought any new clothes in months. She brought me up to date on Dad's latest successes in the garden and then said he was thinking of getting another shoal of discus fish.

'Why does he keep getting those stupid fish?' I asked irritably. 'They only die on him!'

'I don't know,' Mum sighed. 'But he won't give up. He'll manage it one day.'

We walked into a clean and well-ordered reception area and Mum gave her name to the woman at the desk. There were pot plants in one corner and, in another, out-of-date magazines on a low table. I shuffled through the selection – the latest one I could find was already nine months old. We sat in silence as I flicked through my well-worn copy of *Reveal*.

At around 4 p.m. we were shown into the small, tidy office of a psychiatric nurse who had the job of assessing my mother's suitability for disability living allowance. The nurse was a plump, breathless woman in her mid-forties with a kind, if tired, face. She invited us both to sit down and then introduced herself as Cynthia.

'I'm so sorry to have to bring this all up again, Mrs Kelly,' she addressed herself to my mum. 'I know this is incredibly hard for you but it is necessary for the purposes of this assessment. Are you okay with that?'

Mum folded her arms stoically and nodded.

'And you are . . . ?' Cynthia's voice trailed off as she looked at me. She wore round wire-framed glasses and a smile of professional sympathy.

'I'm Jen,' I told her simply. 'This is my mum.'

'Ah, okay.' Cynthia's eyes creased and she made a little note on the top of her form. 'Jen – are you familiar with your mother's background?'

'I . . . eh . . . er . . .' I didn't know how to answer. The truth was that I didn't know much at all beyond the basic facts. But it was uncomfortable to admit this to a stranger, like I didn't really know my mum.

'No,' Mum jumped in. 'She hasn't heard much. I haven't told her.'

'Okay.' Cynthia turned back to my mum. 'Well, look, let's get going, shall we? I understand this goes back to your earliest childhood . . .'

Mum breathed in hard through her nose and looked up

to the ceiling as if steeling herself for a long, uphill climb, then she started: 'They called me Monkey Face . . .'

And that's when it all came out. For the first time in my life, I heard about my mother's truly appalling childhood. I heard about her abusive mother and her absent father, the poverty, the overdoses watched by her and her siblings, the spells in various orphanages until the time the children were made wards of the state and sent to St Grace's. Then I learned of the terrible abuses that went on there. I heard about what they did to my mother and other children in horrible, graphic detail; the beatings, sexual abuse, the daily ritual humiliations. Then I learned about the children returning to the family home, the way my gran forced my mum to work at thirteen, the way she beat her with a metal chain. And then the rape, my mother's abusive first marriage and how she finally escaped to England with my dad to get away from my gran.

All the way through, I sat with my hand over my mouth, unable to take it all in: the broken arms as a baby, the abuse with the nappy pins, the suicide attempt at seven . . . it was too much. My head swam and my heart broke. I had no idea how much time had passed when Mum stopped speaking. She was just in the middle of describing her breakdown after the Redress Board, telling Cynthia about hearing her mother's voice coming out of my father, when suddenly I was aware of an oppressive silence hanging heavily in the air. I wanted to move but I was hyper aware of disturbing the awful stillness.

Then Cynthia spoke: 'And how long after that episode did you hear the voices for?'

All this time, she had been scribbling furiously in her notebook so she didn't see my mother's face when she asked that question.

Mum's eyes filled with tears and she swallowed hard.

'How long?' Mum repeated, her gaze fixed somewhere far away.

'Yes, how long?'

After another pause, Mum answered, 'I still hear them sometimes. Not as much as before. Not all the time and they don't come from Matt any more. But they're there. They never really went away.'

Cynthia put her pen down and looked up at Mum, who had pulled out a hanky and was dabbing at the underside of her eyes. *She still hears voices?* I couldn't believe it.

Cynthia turned to me then and, in a soft voice, she said, 'This must be very hard for you.'

'I didn't know until now,' I whispered and then I broke down sobbing. The things my mum had been through in her life were terrible, so shocking. All of a sudden I was consumed with guilt. How could I have been such a horrible daughter? She didn't deserve the way I had treated her! She didn't deserve any of it. I wanted to say something but I didn't feel it was my place. This was a psychiatric assessment, I was only really there as an observer. *Why? Why hadn't she told me any of this before now?*

Cynthia asked a few more questions about my mother's current situation and she explained that she was still taking antidepressants and seeing a counsellor regularly. She also had monthly appointments with her GP.

When it came time to leave, I felt as if I was walking out of that office a different person. Just a couple of hours before, I had known nothing about my mother. I almost held her in contempt for being unable to function in the normal world. Now I was reeling from the revelations about her life, and full of remorse for how I had treated her all these years.

We left in silence, but the moment we got out of the building I turned to her and, for the first time in as long as I could remember, I gave her a hug. I needed to touch her, to make her know that I loved her. And again, the tears sprung to my eyes.

'I'm sorry,' I whispered. 'I'm so, so sorry.'

'No, it's my fault,' she replied in a low, trembling voice. 'I should have told you earlier. It was just very hard to say.'

'No, Mum,' I insisted. 'I'm sorry for the way that I treated you. I've been a horrible daughter.'

And then I started to sob.

Now it was Mum's turn to comfort me – she pulled me

away from her so that we were face to face. She looked me in the eyes and gripped my shoulders firmly.

'Don't be so silly,' she said. 'You're just a normal teenage girl. Every daughter has arguments with her mum. None of this was anything to do with you. I would have told you sooner, I just didn't know how.'

From that day on, things changed between Mum and me. For the first time, I understood what had made her the person that she was and I started to gain a new respect for her. She had survived the worst that life could throw at anyone and yet she had broken the cycle of abuse to bring us up in the right way. The resentment I'd held against my parents for not giving me the childhood I craved melted away. I had been so desperate to get away from them and felt so aggrieved at all their strict rules, I had no idea they had fought so hard to give me the childhood they had been denied!

Two months later, when my relationship with Arnie crumbled to pieces, I called my parents, begging them to take me home.

'I can't do it any more,' I told Mum on the phone. 'I can't get out of bed.'

For the first time in years I felt like a child again, and my parents swung into action and rescued me. Mum and Dad packed up all my stuff and moved me back home. When

I really needed them, they were there for me. They always had been, I guess, I just didn't know it.

In the first couple of weeks Mum made a big effort, cooking nice home-made stew for me and talking to me about my work at college. Dad did his best but I don't think he realized just how independent I had become. One night, after a particularly fierce row over which channel to watch, Dad snapped, 'This is my house and if you don't like what we're watching you know where you can go. To your room!'

I stormed upstairs, angry with myself for being back in this position again. Angry at him for so many reasons! Mum came up half an hour later and knocked tentatively on the door before sitting down on the end of my bed.

'Don't be angry with your father . . .' she started.

But I was already ranting. 'You know if he had got off his arse to go to work he could have prepared for my future and saved some money so that I didn't have to go to work all the time. I mean, he wants me in education but then he doesn't make it easy for me! I've had to do everything myself. EVERYTHING! It's not like he's got any other children! I'm it!'

'Your father is doing his best,' Mum sighed. 'But you know, you already have so much more than he had as a child. You're a lucky girl. I wish you could see that.'

'It doesn't feel like it sometimes.' I looked away, my eyes

now filling with tears. 'I mean, sometimes it feels like he doesn't even want me around.'

'You know why he didn't come to help you move in with Arnie?'

'Because he couldn't be bothered?' I said bitterly.

'No,' Mum reproached me gently. 'Because he was too upset that you were leaving.'

'Really?'

Mum nodded and touched a hand to my shoulder. 'You know he can't say these things. But that doesn't mean he doesn't feel them.'

After that, I tried to be a bit more considerate around my father. It helped that I didn't have the pressure of trying to pay the bills, I had more time to relax and give my degree my full attention. I was also grateful for the opportunity to get closer to Mum again. Now that I knew what she had been through, I had a new appreciation and respect for her. So instead of walking away when I caught her crying, I'd give her a hug and make her a cup of tea. I'd remind her that she was a strong woman and she always had me to talk to. I would always be there for her.

Now, when we were alone together, I asked her questions and encouraged her to talk about her life. I started to understand the roots of the strict regime that she had instilled in our household and to see where all her anger came from. One thing I knew for a fact, it wasn't from me. She loved me and I knew it now. It was just that she was tormented by the painful memories of her past. One day she told me she was trying to write a book about her experiences and I thought that was a fantastic idea so I encouraged her to keep going.

Meanwhile, I was finding ways to reconnect with my dad too. I don't know why but with every year that had passed we had grown further and further apart. When I was a little girl we had been inseparable, always painting, gardening or doing woodwork together, but as I got older, he closed himself off from me until we could no longer communicate properly. I wanted to get back to how things were. So one day, when he said he was going to the garden centre to buy some seeds, I offered to go with him.

'Ah now, you don't really want to come, do you?' he said dismissively.

'Why not?' I replied. 'I could give you a lift if you like?'

Dad had given up his car many years before when they could no longer afford the running costs. Now he paused to consider my proposal. Finally he nodded. 'Sure. Why not?'

We didn't talk much on the way down but once we were there, it was like my dad came alive. He started chatting animatedly about planting, soils and seeds, and the words just seemed to tumble out of him.

We walked up and down the rows of different compost bags and he stopped at each one to explain the type of compost we would need for our soil and the vegetables he was growing. I listened carefully and asked questions, and for the first time in years it felt like we were having a normal, natural conversation. I don't think he had any idea how happy it made me.

On the way back, I worked up the courage to ask a question which I knew would make him uncomfortable.

'Dad, I didn't get to meet Grandpa – what was he like?'

'What? My father?' Dad was visibly shocked. I *never* asked questions like this usually. But I'd decided I'd had enough of secrets and hiding.

'Yes, your father. My grandfather.'

Silence. I was grateful at that moment to be driving so I had something to distract me from the intense quietness in the car.

'Well, you *did* meet him actually,' he said eventually. 'I introduced you to him when you were just a baby but he wasn't really into babies all that much. Do you know what your grandfather was?'

'Was he a bank robber, Daddy?'

A slight pause and, a second later, I caught my dad's eye. We both burst out laughing – it felt so surreal, so silly to say those words, and yet we both knew that it was the absolute truth. Over the years I had picked up various bits and pieces from my siblings and my aunts about my dad's side of the family. He thought he'd been so smart in hiding it from me but I knew they were all criminals. I just didn't know anything from Dad directly.

'That's right,' he said. 'He was a robber, but you don't really want to know about all of this, do you?'

'Yes, I do!' I insisted. 'I really want to know. It's my family too.'

Gradually, Dad started to open up. It wasn't easy – he had been trained to keep his mouth shut from when he was just a little boy. They all had to abide by the 'code', it was drummed into them – and as a result Dad became secretive. Even though he had lived a straight and clean life for over fifteen years, he still found it hard to talk about his life before coming to England. Instinctively, he kept that part of himself hidden.

'I don't know why you want to know these things,' he'd bluster whenever I brought it up. 'It's all ancient history. What's the point of raking it up?'

'Because I'm curious! I'm allowed to be curious, you know.'

'Well, curiosity killed the cat.'

'We don't have a cat.'

'Don't be a smart mouth!'

The one thing I could never get him to talk about was the heroin. Since Dad took methadone, I knew he must have been an addict at one time but I could sense he was deeply ashamed of this and the subject made him uncomfortable. One day I asked him how long he had been clean and he visibly bristled. Then he said to me, 'Look, Jen, I wasn't proud of meself when I was doing it. It's in the past now and that's where I want it to stay. You're my daughter and the way I've lived my life, well, I've tried to lead by example.

'You want to know what your grandfather was like? He did an awful lot of talking – saying a lot of stuff and then doing the opposite. As your father, I didn't always say the right thing but I tried to do the right thing. And that's the most important part of being a parent to me. After that, well, nobody does everything right! So you can ask me all these things but I'm not always going to tell you. I was there for you, that's all you need to know.'

True to form, on my graduation day my parents turned up but Dad never said a word to me. I knew deep down he was proud that I got a 2:1 but it hurt that he couldn't bring himself to say 'well done'. And when I should have been bursting with pride and happiness, I felt a bitter twisting in my guts.

'What's wrong?' Mum asked.

'Nothing,' I huffed.

'No, go on, what is it? You shouldn't be upset today, not today.'

'Oh, I don't know, Mum! It's just that after all these years of being a good daughter, doing what I was told and not being able to go out, I did it! I got my education, I can get a good job now. You got what you wanted as parents, didn't you? So where's the "well done"?'

'You know I'm proud of you,' she replied, a little wounded.

'I know *you* are,' I said pointedly, staring at Dad who was stood separately from the crowds. Mum nodded and went over to speak to him. It seemed she dragged him back, reluctantly, a few minutes later. We stood around in expectant silence for a while, then Mum sighed and rolled her eyes.

'Well?' she asked him impatiently. 'Are you not going to say well done to her?'

Dad caught my eye briefly and grunted something that sounded like: 'El un.' And then he walked away. Mum grinned at me triumphantly, as if she had just performed a minor miracle. I shrugged. I suppose it was good enough. At least he tried.

Now I've moved in with my boyfriend Lucas and we're saving up to get married. From the word go, it had felt very natural and easy – as if we were always meant to be together. He has a daughter who he is so loving and gentle with that I can see he's a brilliant dad, which makes me really excited about having children together one day. His daughter is a very special little girl and, luckily, we get on really well when she stays at the weekends. I can honestly say I'm happier than I've ever been in my life.

Even Dad gets on with Lucas, something I never expected. I reminded Dad that he stopped me going out with him when I was fourteen, but he only saw this as an example of his excellent parenting skills. 'You see!' he said. 'If I'd let you go out with him at that age you wouldn't have gone to university, you would have got distracted, maybe had a child together, struggled, split up and moved on. You were far too young back then. No, I was quite right, Jen. Look at you both now – so happy together. I think you should thank me for doing you a big favour!'

'Urgh! Dad – you're impossible!' I laughed, throwing a cushion at his head.

'It's true!'

'Yeah, whatever . . .'

But I can see that in some ways my dad was right. I got my education because he was strict with me – other friends didn't do so well. Helen, whose parents were both addicts, dropped out of school when she fell pregnant. Today she's got four kids from three different fathers and struggles to get by on her benefits. At twenty-two she's never had a job and I wonder if she ever will. I don't judge her for the choices she's made – in some ways, I wonder if they were her choices at all. She didn't have the benefit of what I had. She created a large family so that she would never be lonely. I understand that.

I have a great job now as a laboratory research assistant and I hope to do well in my profession so that I can build a strong career. But I also want kids – I dream one day of owning a beautiful house filled with noisy, boisterous children. In short, I want what I didn't have and, like my dad said, thanks to his strict rules I can have it. Lucas and I have even talked about moving to Ireland one day; though he is not from Ireland himself, and has never been before, he has an Irish father so he's part-Irish. I know that it would break my heart to leave my parents but I would love for my kids to grow up with their cousins. My great hope is that one day Mum and Dad decide to move back too, though I know it will take a lot to convince them.

It's ironic that they came over to England to give me a better life and now I yearn to return to Ireland, but I can't help it. That's where all my family lives and because they are there it is where I feel most at home. Dad doesn't want to go back, though – most of his family are recovering addicts and criminals still, and every year he gets a phone call from one of his brothers telling him another member of their family has died. He escaped that life and the idea of returning frightens him. But would it be the same after all this time?

At least we're having the conversation now. At least we are talking like a family – planning the future and sharing the past. I even know that somewhere out there I have a half-sister called Felicity. We've never met but I'd like to one day, and I hope she'd like to meet me too. It's strange to think that somewhere in the world there is another girl who shares my dad's genes. How ironic that after all these years praying for a sibling my own age I had one all along! I think about Felicity often, wondering what she looks like and what she's doing. One day, if she hasn't come looking for me, I'll try and get in touch. I have so much to tell her!

Today my mother is coping a lot better. Although she still takes medication, has house visits from social workers and attends a psychiatric hospital, I see her happy days more. Watching her go through a life of silence and pain inspired me to qualify in mental health and social work so that I could help others struggling with their mental well-being.

I can't even begin to describe how much I love and appreciate my mum and dad. They suffered a lot in their lives and my mum, in particular, had a brutal childhood. I am so proud of how she broke the cycle of abuse and neglect to show me the love every child deserves. I don't idolize celebrities or models, she is my idol, my rock. I see how she suffered and survived and for this I am so proud of her. I could wish my mother hadn't gone through this pain, but none of us can change the past. Besides, Mum's struggles have made her the wonderful, sensitive, kind and loving person she is today.

It made her the mother she never had.

22

IRENE

⊥

The Promise
JANUARY 2015

It was on my most recent trip to Ireland that I decided to confront the last ghosts from my past. It had been a blustery, grey day and, for some reason, I couldn't stop thinking about all the children who had left their innocence and childhood at the gates of that orphanage. After the Ryan Report came out, the world was shocked at the sheer scale of the abuse in the orphanages. It was like the Catholic Church had created a whole generation of lost children and now, whenever I returned to Dublin, I felt like reaching out and touching strangers to ask them: *Was it you too? Did they do these things to you?* I examined the faces of the people who passed me in the street, searching for signs that they had known the same pain as me. The odds were on my side – there were so many of us.

I sat in a steamy, crowded cafe, both hands wrapped

round a mug of tea, lost in my thoughts and memories. Philip and I had spent the morning shopping but when the bitter January chill turned my toes numb, I announced it was time for a tea break. The chattering around me faded into the distance as my mind returned once again to the orphanage. All of a sudden, I snapped back to reality.

'Can we go to St Grace's?' I asked Philip. 'I want to see what it looks like now.'

He gave me an uncertain 'okay' but I assured him that I felt strong enough for the visit.

'The damage is done,' I told him. 'There's nothing more those people can do to hurt me. It's over. I just need to see it, that's all.'

Philip drove me to the place I had been desperate to escape from as a child and, as we passed familiar landmarks, visions flashed up in my mind: here was a little girl running down the road, holding her brother and sister's hands, looking back over her shoulder, praying that they weren't being followed. Now I saw a girl in a pretty white communion dress, arm outstretched to grasp the hand of a father she had only just met. We were nearly at the gates when I saw another girl with a young couple, crying and begging not to be taken back inside. Already, I felt a lump in my throat, but I was determined to see this through. You see, a very long time ago I had made a promise to that little girl. I promised that I would find a way to free her.

As we turned off the road to go through the large iron

gates, an unexpected sadness swept through my body. The car rolled slowly up the driveway but now, instead of lawns on either side, there were blocks of modern houses, all fresh red bricks and lacquered black doors. I wondered what happened to the horse. The large grey building at the end was still there and I braced myself as we drove up towards it. As we got closer, I half expected to see a black-and-white habit glide out of the front door to greet us but I knew that St Grace's had been closed now for many years. The scandals had been too much – hundreds of survivors from this place had come forward to give evidence against the nuns and staff. So many lost souls, so many ruined childhoods.

I got out of the car slowly and my eyes swept up and down the building – it seemed exactly as it was all those years ago except now the windows were boarded up, and I was dismayed to see large padlocks on the front door. I walked towards it but Philip touched my arm.

'You can't go in, Mum,' he said softly. 'Look! It's padlocked.'

'But . . . but I have to go in. There's something I have to do.'

Philip shook his head. 'It's not possible.'

'Check it, Philip! Please, for me, just check the lock and see if it can be opened.'

He frowned and let out a sigh but he went to the door and checked the padlock, just as I asked. Then he went through the metal chain link by link with his hands to see if there were any breaks and even tugged at the front doors to see if they would give a little. But nothing – I could see it was useless. The door was firmly locked and suddenly I was overcome with frustration.

'Damn it!' I said through gritted teeth.

'They're building houses here, Mum,' Philip called, pointing to a large glossy billboard advertising a new housing estate for the site. The hand-drawn picture showed an idyllic set of large houses with happy cartoon people coming and going. He wandered further away, towards the back of the building.

'The back of it is gone completely,' he called again. 'It's all been pulled down.'

So St Grace's was gone – in reality, I was just looking at a facade, a crumbling memory of a place that no longer existed. I closed my eyes then, let my chin sink down, and I gave in to the tears. Hugging myself, my shoulders shaking, I let all the sadness flow out of me. Philip was quickly at my side, putting his arms round me, and we stayed like that for a while.

'I wanted to go inside . . .' I started then stopped as the tears overtook me again.

'I know, I know, Mum,' he whispered. Now the wind was stronger and it blew an icy chill through me. The tears stung my cheeks.

'Oh God, it's freezing,' I said as I finally pulled myself away and attempted to dry my face. I looked around and, for the first time, I saw there were a few people standing in the doorways and front gardens of the houses. Even from a distance I could see their eyes were full of sympathy and understanding.

'I can't have been the first,' I whispered to Philip. 'They must have had lots of visits like this.'

'Who would want to live here?' he said. 'Do you not think it would be too sad to live in these grounds?'

'People need houses,' I rebuked him gently. 'And it's better they do something positive with this place, something that will help people. I'd hate to think of it standing here, abandoned forever, like some bloody monument to misery.'

'I suppose so.' Philip smiled at me now. The old mum was back. 'Come on,' he said. 'Are you ready to go home now?'

It has been a long and difficult journey back to health since my last and worst breakdown, the time when I had to go into respite care. Luckily, I have had fantastic support from an assortment of doctors, nurses, therapists, psychiatrists and counsellors, people who have helped me every step of the way. All my life I tried to lock away the memories of what happened to me in St Grace's, to push them down so that I wouldn't have to face them. But once I gave my evidence, I had no control over them any more. I couldn't lock them away. My head was chaos, a complete mess, and

I couldn't focus on anything. Voices and visions were with me all the time and fighting them simply didn't work any more.

I'd be walking down the street when I'd hear my mother's voice in my ear, *Things aren't going to be good for very long, we're coming to get you.*

'Go away!' I'd reply out loud, as if talking to a real person. 'Just let me do my shopping in peace. I don't want to listen to you.'

We're going to bring you down. You're a horrible, evil person . . .

'I don't want to hear it! You're not real!'

I AM REAL!

The more I argued, the louder her voice got so I got louder too. It came to a point where I was having full-blown rows with myself in the street.

But with all the counselling I've been given better tools for coping with the voices when they come back, which they still do when I'm having an off day. Now, instead of arguing with them or trying to deny their reality, I listen to them and then I dismiss them. I'm not running away and hiding any more, I'm choosing to face my fears and tackle them head on. It's not always easy but it's working a lot better than anything else I have tried. I've also learned how to meditate and visualize things in a calm, positive way.

I still write – poetry works like a pressure valve for me, it releases these intense emotions in little bursts, taking the stress out of my head and giving me some breathing space.

I used to write in the dark with my music – it was my way of drowning out the voices – but today I write any time of the day or night.

Every Monday, I have two hours of counselling. I see my GP once a month, my psychiatrist once every four months and I have access to a twenty-four-hour crisis line. It is a great comfort that I can use this service any time and someone will come and see me. It all helps to make me feel safe and supported and to carry on with my life. I'm one of the lucky ones, I know that. I survived when so many others didn't.

Best of all, I have Matt. For the last twenty-five years he has been my rock, never leaving me, never denying what I told him. Each time I fell apart, he held me in his arms until I calmed down. His strength pulled me through. There were times I felt tremendous guilt because I knew that he struggled to keep his head above water, he was lost in my pain, not knowing what to do or who to turn to for help. But just holding and comforting me was all I needed from him at that time. He couldn't solve my problems – all he could do was help me through them. And he did.

I have Jennifer's support too, which is something I never imagined. Most of her life I tried to hide the truth from her, but I see now that the hiding itself became a source of pain to her. She was lonely and confused and she had no idea why I struggled so much. I just wish there had been another way but I didn't know how to cope myself. I had spent so long hiding behind closed doors, I didn't know how to open them. It took a complete crisis for us to learn how to trust each other. Now, when I'm having a bad day, she sits down next to me and we talk. I can see she wants to help and it means so much that she wants to be there for me. I feel blessed to have her.

The irony is that Jennifer saved both our lives before she was even born. I am in no doubt whatsoever that, if I hadn't fallen pregnant with her, I would never have survived another ten years in Ireland. Nor Matt for that matter. That's why I had a big party when I reached fifty. It was a miracle to me that I lived so long! I'm so proud of Jen and I know that she has found her soulmate. If she is quiet and introverted sometimes, I have only myself to blame. It is probably a habit she has picked up from Matt and me. I just hope that she finds a way of dealing with her problems, even if she doesn't want to talk to her mum about them.

Despite the difficult time they had growing up, my other children have turned out to be such well-balanced, decent people, and I'm proud of them all. All three of them are excellent parents and their lives revolve around their kids. My grandchildren are amazing young things – very happy, always smiling and laughing. It's just the way it should be.

For a long time, I felt that the injustice of what happened to all us survivors was insurmountable. That I would never get over what they did to us or how they protected the perpetrators from facing up to their crimes. Today, I still get angry about what happened, but I refuse to let it define me. In this way, I've started the important process of healing. Writing this book has been part of that process, because as a child I was denied a voice. It wasn't just the nuns, it was everyone – our families, doctors, teachers, the Garda, the whole of Irish society. Nobody would hear a word against them, nobody dare question them. They held all the power while vulnerable children like myself were helpless to defend ourselves.

But they can't hurt me any more – I refuse to let them. And in writing this book, I am defying their order to stay silent. Because, as a society, we can't afford to forget the wrongs that were done in the name of Christianity, we can't let one part of society become so powerful again that they are free to do whatever they like. But more than that, I wrote this book as a testimony to those children who were abused and didn't make it. I still hear them today – at night, when it's very quiet, I can hear the sound of babies crying. The babies from the nursery, the ones I couldn't help.

I am sitting cross-legged on the floor in my bedroom and I am breathing in the way I've been taught. In through the nose and out through the mouth, focusing on inhaling and exhaling slowly and steadily. I close my eyes and turn my mind to the way the air flows into and out of my body. I tune in to myself, listening to my own breathing until it is the only sound I can hear. I let my mind go blank and still.

There is darkness, a cold hollow darkness. I wait for the pictures to form themselves around me, and then, out of the inky blackness, the shape of the corridor begins to grow around my body. Hard stone floor, tall ceilings, and walls that accelerate away from me. At the very end, I see the girl on the floor, just where I left her, crying.

The corridor seems longer and darker than ever before but today I won't leave her. I start to walk towards her now – at first my limbs feel heavy and slow, as if I am a giant in a storybook, cumbersome and huge, striding forward in slow motion. It takes every ounce of strength to lift each leaden foot and place it in front of the other, but I won't give up. I have come back to get her, just as I promised.

The darkness is like a fierce wind that pushes against me, resisting me, refusing to let me past, but I push back and gradually the distance between the girl and me shortens. Now I am closer, I can see the worn buckles on her shoes, the knots in her hair and the rips in her dress. Still, she hides her face and cries. The wind against me eases, and with every step I feel myself growing in strength and confidence. My feet are lighter now, my step firmer, and I move more quickly until I am stood right there next to her and she turns her tear-stained face up to me.

'*Here, come with me.*' I reach out and take her hand. '*This time we can go.*'

We start walking back down the corridor towards the door . . .

I say, '*It's time to meet your children and your grandchildren, the people you created . . .*'

She is beside me and we are getting closer to the door which radiates light . . .

'*Because this is you now. This is the woman you are today. You're standing tall. You've come through this and no one is going to hurt you again. I love you.*'

Together we walk through the open door into the sunlight, and a bright burst of whiteness blinds my vision. I look down again and the girl is gone. She is free.

Acknowledgements

FROM IRENE:

I would like to thank my lovely GP who got me the help I needed, the doctors, nurses and social workers from the hospital, my counsellor – who is a wonderful lady – and most important of all, all the people who helped me get this book out there – thank you all so much! And thanks to Matt and my wonderful children for making my life better.

FROM JENNIFER:

Growing up was sometimes hard and very lonely, but as I've grown older and got to know my brothers and sister, they have become more than my siblings, they are my best friends. They are my escape, my safe place when I need a break. I am so proud that they are my family because without them there would be something missing in my heart.

My dad was and always will be my first love. As a child I adored him, despite his lack of affection. I didn't understand why back then but today I realize it's because, although he didn't hug me or tuck me in at night, he never left my side. He left a whole life behind for me and most of all he saved my mum from a life she thought she would never escape.

Although I don't follow him around with the same puppy dog eyes, I respect and love him. I am proud of the changes he made to better himself because without those changes I wouldn't have achieved what I have in life.

My mother will never truly know how much I love her. She is my inspiration, she is my entire world. At the age of twenty-two I still call her when I'm sick or upset and she never turns me away. She scoops me up as if I was a baby again and in that moment everything is okay. I'm so proud of her for everything she has achieved. There is nothing that gives me more happiness in this world than when I look at my mum and she is happy. She deserves the world and I'll never give up trying to give it to her.

Lastly, Katy, I never thought my mum would get her chance to tell her story and like a little ray of sunshine on a miserable day you appeared. You have given my mum more than anything in this world, you have given her a voice and now she can release her demons. You'll never truly know what you have done for us and we will never forget you. You are a true friend for life, thank you.

Information and Advice

The Ryan Report is available to read and download at:
www.childabusecommission.ie

Amnesty International Ireland's 2011 report *In Plain Sight*, which assessed the abuse of Irish children in State institutions, and the State's responses to them, against the standards dictated by international human rights law, is available at: www.amnesty.ie/content/plain-sight

IRISH SURVIVORS IN BRITAIN
Support for Irish survivors of institutional abuse
living in Britain:
www.irishsurvivorsinbritain.org

JUSTICE FOR MAGDALENES
Promotes and represents the interests of Magdalene survivors:
www.magdalenelaundries.com

MIND
Offers support, information and guidance on all issues
relating to mental health:
www.mind.org.uk

To read some of Irene Kelly's poetry please visit her web-page: poeticpicturesirenekelly.wordpress.com

For more information about Katy Weitz visit: www.ghost-writer4hire.org